# GLEANING IN ANCIENT FIELDS

## A Christian's Guide to the First Five Books of the Bible

**Maxine Carlill**

WESTBOW
PRESS®
A DIVISION OF THOMAS NELSON
& ZONDERVAN

WestBow Press books may be ordered through booksellers or by contacting:

WestBow Press
A Division of Thomas Nelson & Zondervan
1663 Liberty Drive
Bloomington, IN 47403
www.westbowpress.com
1 (866) 928-1240

ISBN: 978-1-9736-8622-4 (sc)
ISBN: 978-1-9736-8623-1 (e)

Print information available on the last page.

WestBow Press rev. date: 3/10/2020

# INTRODUCTION

2 Timothy 3:16 declares: *"**All scripture** is given by inspiration of God, and is profitable for doctrine, for reproof, for correction, for instruction in righteousness."*

This declaration, stated before there was a New Testament, is referring to the Hebrew Scriptures which we call the Old Testament and includes the First Five Books of Moses – the Torah. Yet these Books are often neglected or thought to be no longer relevant. It is true that much of what we think of as 'law' was meant for the Jewish people alone who are called to obey the details spelt out through Moses. However, embedded within these Books are <u>patterns, principles and pictures</u> that the Torah Giver intended for all to follow. This book is to help you discover them.

Like Ruth, the Gentile girl from Moab for whom the fields of Boaz provided sustenance, Gentile Believers in the God of Israel can glean in Jewish fields. In this book, you will be introduced to Jewish scholarship which over the centuries, has explored every nuance of meaning of God's words to His Covenant people. These studies will also show how the teaching of Torah flows throughout the New Testament.

The teaching contained in this book may be used as a guide to further Bible Study. It is by no means comprehensive but written with the hope that as Christians read the first five books of the Bible, they will do so with a deeper appreciation and understanding.

# CONTENTS

### Gems from Genesis:

This chapter contains some highlights, 'gems', from this important Book of Beginnings. In it we see God beginning the pattern of dividing and separating and setting the scene for His chosen people to emerge.

### The Elegance of Exodus:

Elegance is a theme through this book, as God lifts the lowly to exalted positions. Luke 1:52

### Lessons of Leviticus:

This is the Book of Holiness. Out of all the 'rules and regulations', what is meant for the non-Jewish believer in order to follow a Holy God?

## Wisdom from the Wilderness:

There were victories but also failures as the people of God began their journey towards the goal of entering into all that God had promised them. Finally, the wisdom of obeying and trusting became clear to this band of pilgrims.

## Directions from Deuteronomy:

Their Teacher and Deliverer was soon going to die but had many more instructions for his beloved nation before they entered the Promised Land without his leadership. His words can equip us to take hold of all God has for us.

# NOTE

The names of people and places have been Hebraised to emphasise the Hebraic setting of the Bible. Note that '*ch*' in Hebrew words generally make the guttural sound of the Hebrew letter, 'het'.

Footnotes are included to give explanations of unfamiliar references or words.

Scriptures quoted are from the NKJV (used with permission), unless otherwise stated.

It is advisable to have your Bible open at the particular Book being studied. References to that Book are generally not quoted. However, most Scripture references from elsewhere in the Bible, are.

The author may be contacted at mjcarlill@gmail.com

# ACKNOWLEDGEMENTS

I wish to thank my husband Jim for his support, encouragement and assistance. Thank you to the many friends who encouraged me to go ahead with a book on this subject.

Thank you for assistance from Cecile, Corrie, Dianne, Heather and Teri.

I am grateful for the connection to Jewish teaching and traditions I have had while living in Israel. I am particularly thankful to Rabbi Yakov Youlus, who until his death taught Torah to Christians, in spite of criticism from his peers for doing so. He showed me hidden treasures and taught me how to begin to discover its messages, may his memory be blessed. These First Five Books I believe are the foundation to all that follows in the Word of God.

# GEMS FROM GENESIS

Genesis means 'beginnings', as does *Bereshit*, the Hebrew name of the first Book of the Torah. And immediately in the beginning, we see patterns beginning to emerge. The following are 'gems', some highlights, that demonstrate some of these important patterns as well as principles and pictures that God has embedded in the Torah.

## Genesis 1
### God's Sovereignty Established

In the first chapter, the fact there was a creation, and therefore a Creator, gives us a meaning to life. A Torah Scholar, Rabbi Yeruchem Levovitch[1] explains:

'From the first verse (of Genesis) as soon as you start studying Torah, right from the first verse you become aware that there is a Creator and Ruler of the universe. This first awareness already makes a major change in you for the rest of your life. You realize that there is a reason for everything. The world has meaning and purpose. Without meaning there is no real enjoyment or satisfaction'.

---

[1] (ca. 1873-1936) R. Levovitch was the spiritual leader of a great Yeshiva (Torah and Talmudic Learning Centre) in Poland.

He goes on to say that those who believe in the Creator see His handiwork everywhere, and concludes:

'This is the profound message of the first verse of the Torah!'

Romans 1:20-32 affirms that Creation should indeed result in awareness of a Creator. Verse 20 says, *"For since the creation of the world His invisible attributes are clearly seen, being understood by the things that are made,* even *His eternal power and Godhead, so that they are without excuse."* However, the passage goes on to state, although man is without excuse because creation clearly demonstrates the existence of a Creator, he has suppressed truth and the consequences of that have led to him being filled with unrighteousness.

Not only does the acceptance of a Creator give meaning to life, but God's sovereignty over His creation is established at the moment of that creation. The world is His to do with it as He wants – and to give some of it to whom He wants.

The fact that He is Creator is often referred to in Scripture to confirm His power. For example, in Isaiah 40, God is speaking of His promises of restoration for the nation of Israel. In verse 25-26 God challenges Israel to remember His power (as demonstrated by creation) and therefore His ability to do what He has promised, *"To whom shall I be equal? Lift up your eyes on high,* **and see who has created these things,** *Who brings out their host by number; He calls them all by name, By the greatness of His might And the strength of His power..."*

In Genesis 1:2 we see another attribute of the Creator - how He cares for His creation. We read that the spirit of God was hovering, or as it is sometimes translated, moving. However, the Hebrew word, *merahefet,* means that the hovering, or moving, was a movement of cherishing, of tender love. It is used one other time in Deuteronomy 32:11 which describes the love of a mother eagle for her young.

Just as we see the power and sovereignty of God in His act of creation, we learn in chapter 2:7 that Adam is created out of the dust of the earth, which speaks of frailty. His name, Adam, is connected to the Hebrew word for earth - *'adumah'*. Man has a <u>soul</u> called a *'nephesh'* (which animals also have). In Genesis 2:7 we read that man became, '...a living being/soul/ *nephesh'*. However, most notably, we read also in 2:7, that when he was created, God breathed into him '...the breath/*neshemah* of life...' which sets him apart from other living beings, or creatures.

Before we leave the marvellous account of beginnings, we will look at an example of *Gematria,* a practice in Judaism that assigns the numerical value of each Hebrew letter to a word, name, or phrase, to link those words or phrases to each other. It can reveal hidden lessons and emphasise concepts. Within the creation account from Genesis 1:1-31, *Elohim,* one of the names of God, is mentioned 32 times in the creation. The numerical value for 'heart', in Hebrew *'lev',* is 32. So, say the Jewish sages, just as the heart keeps pumping to keep the body going, God keeps the universe going.

One other thing to note too is that Adam is not only the name of the first man but is the word for a 'human being' in the Bible and is not a plural word - we are all from one ancestor which is why Judaism holds the belief that one day we will all be one.

## Genesis 2
## Dividing and Separating

From the beginning we see a pattern established, that of dividing and separating. This pattern will be pointed out in this Study many times. In the act of creating, God separates light from darkness/*Choshek*, a word that carries in it the sense of misery, destruction, death, ignorance, sorrow, wickedness. It represents spiritual darkness and while God called the light, 'good', He did not call the darkness good. To continue, water was separated from land, and man from the other living creatures. Now in Genesis 2:1-3 God is again separating and setting apart, in this case, a pocket of time - the Seventh Day. Biblically, the number seven represents Divine perfection.

God is sovereign so He can make holy - that is, set apart for Himself, what He wants. He did that to the Seventh Day. God ceased from creative work[2]. It was not because He needed a rest, because as Isaiah 40:28 says, *"Have you not known? Have you not heard? The everlasting God, the LORD, The Creator of the ends of the earth, Neither faints nor is weary."* No, all was done and set in order for the creation to now 'reproduce itself'.

Through the Sabbath He embedded a powerful picture. That of the 'new creation'; the Seventh Day rest speaks of a Rest into

---

[2] The Hebrew word for work in this context is *m'lacah* - and means creative work, rather than physical labour.

which we are invited to enter. Hebrews 4:9-10, *"There remains therefore a rest for the people of God. For he who has entered His rest has himself also ceased from his works as God did from His."* We do not have to work for our redemption but rest in what has been provided for us. This beautiful picture is why later through the Mosaic Law, He gave strict instructions to His 'set apart' people, to keep this day holy.

In the first chapter, it ends each act of creation with, *"...evening and morning it was the (first, second, etc) day..."* This is why the Hebrew calendar starts the new day in the evening.

Shabbat is the only day named – the others are referred to in Hebrew as Day One, Day Two etc. They are a countdown to Shabbat.

Because Shabbat is linked with creation, it is a day of remembering that there is a Creator. From Charles Darwin on though, there has been no Creator in the minds of many people. Therefore, there is no-one in control and no instructions that need to be heeded. Again, note Romans 1:20 quoted in the beginning of this Study, the evidence of a Creator is clearly demonstrated leaving no excuse for denying His existence.

Later, God sets aside other spaces in time and calls them holy and gives them to His people, designating them as 'appointments with the LORD'. The Hebrew word for these occasions is *moad* which means – an appointed time or meeting - and first appears in the plural in Genesis 1:14 where it is usually translated as 'signs and seasons'. In Leviticus 23:1-2, it speaks of *"...the feasts (moadim/appointments) of the LORD..."* The Rabbis say though, that the weekly festival of Shabbat is the foremost of the festivals, it is a weekly appointment with God. In observant Jewish households today, Shabbat is a time of disconnecting from the world and connecting to God and family. The home and meals are prepared in advance in order to honour this day.

## Genesis 3
## Whose Will?

God made man to have free will which made him different from the animals. Man had the ability to choose between right or wrong. In Genesis 2:17, God gives Adam and Eve one commandment, *"but of the tree of the knowledge of good and evil you shall not eat."* In this First Test of whether to obey God or give in to fleshly desires, the flesh won. The senses were gratified.

Note: Eve (in Hebrew – *Chava,*) 'saw' it was good. Usually, only taste will tell if a fruit is good or not, but her thoughts and imagination did the rest. The test was about self-restraint, and it involved food, and both she and her husband failed.

The first temptation in the wilderness of Yeshua[3] was whether to eat and therefore break his fast or not – Luke 4:3 *"...command this stone to become bread."*

God's instructions given at Sinai were to ensure that His people would live holy lives to reflect His holiness. They included instructions about food. Self-restraint had to be exercised in

---

[3] Jesus' Hebrew name

order to obey them. Note that in Jewish tradition, potential health benefits that may come from restraining from unclean foods are not considered the reason for following the relative commandments. They are simply counted among the laws which do not necessarily have rational explanations but are to be obeyed anyway because God has so commanded it.

The spirit obeys God, but the flesh wants its own way. The senses of the flesh were involved in the sin of Adam and Chava, they listened, they saw, they touched, they tasted. Romans 8:5 speaks of living according to the flesh or the spirit. *"For those who live according to the flesh set their minds on the things of the flesh, but those who live according to the Spirit, the things of the Spirit."* By which will we be navigated?

Rabbi Jonathan Sacks[4] says that:

'The sin of the first humans in the Garden of Eden was that they followed their eyes, not their ears. Their actions were determined by what they saw, the beauty of the tree, not by what they heard, namely the word of God commanding them not to eat from it'.

It's interesting that when the couple hid from God, it was because of their **shame** of being found naked, not from **guilt** of disobedience to the One with whom they fellowshipped.

Shame is what we feel when we don't live up to what we think others expect of us. Guilt is used by our conscience to remind us of what is really right and wrong according to God's standards.

---

[4] Chief Rabbi of the United Hebrew Congregations in the UK from 1991 to 2013

In Genesis 3:9, God asks His first question of man, 'Where are you?' Admission of guilt was drawn out, but with excuses justifying their actions. The heart of God still asks the same question and man still justifies his disobedience.

Adam and Chava made an effort to cover their nakedness, (Genesis 3:7). Nakedness represents being without the covering and protection of God. Man's own efforts to cover shame are futile though. When the prophet Isaiah speaks of Israel's sin in turning away from God he says in 59:6, *"Their webs will not become garments, Nor will they cover themselves with their works; Their works* are *works of iniquity, And the act of violence* is *in their hands."* And in Revelation 3:17-18, the church of Sardis was rebuked for not realising they were naked and were exhorted, *"I counsel you to buy from Me gold refined in the fire, that you may be rich; and white garments, that you may be clothed, that the shame of your nakedness may not be revealed."*

There are various scriptures throughout the Bible that use the analogy of clothing to portray a spiritual truth. Only God can cover our 'nakedness' before Him, and there in *Gan Eden* (the Garden of Eden) He provided the covering for Adam and Chava, *"...the LORD God made tunics of skin, and clothed them."* It seems that in this place of beauty and provision, the first innocent life was sacrificed to cover the shame and the vulnerability that sin brought, (Genesis 3:21). It is to be noted though, that the scriptural record does not actually record that God killed an animal to provide those garments. The first recorded death is that of Abel by his brother's hand.

## Genesis 4 & 5
## Repentance and Forgiveness

Cain's (*Kayin*) name is a play on the word 'to acquire'. This is reflected in Chava's statement made at her first son's birth, 'I have gained/acquired man'. His brother's name was Abel/*Hevel* and it means, 'breath or vapour'. It was Hevel who brought the more acceptable sacrifice. Genesis 4:3-4, *"And in the process of time it came to pass that Cain brought an offering of the fruit of the ground to the LORD. Abel also brought of the firstborn of his flock and of their fat. And the LORD respected Abel and his offering."* The Jewish sages derive from this passage, that Kayin's sacrifice may have been from inferior produce as it is implied in the Hebrew that Hevel's sacrifice was from the firstborn and the choicest. Note that the word translated '*...and of their fat*' can mean choicest or finest. Also, it is possible that Kayin's offering came from the ground that was cursed (Genesis 3:17) rather than purchasing an animal to offer as a burnt offering. Kayin's attitude was also rejected by the LORD who warned him to rule over his sinful inclination. The principle that man will be forgiven through repentance, was firmly established in this incident. However, sin unchecked leads to worse behaviour and in this chapter, the first murder was committed.

## Genesis 6
## Relevant Righteousness

Verses 11 and 12 of chapter 6 are among the saddest in the entire Bible. Genesis 6:11 tells us, *"The earth also was corrupt before God, and the earth was filled with violence."*

The word translated as 'corrupt', means ruin, something perverted. In ten generations the world had gone from 'very good', Genesis 1:31, to ruin.

Luke 17:26, *"And as it was in the days of Noah, so it will be also in the days of the Son of Man."* Although in this verse Yeshua emphasises the total unawareness by the population of coming judgement, the days of Noah are known by the Jewish Sages as days of violence towards each other, the total collapse of moral standards, degeneracy and shamelessness.

We know one man was righteous. However, we can stop and note here, that Jewish and Christian perceptions sometimes differ!

Noah comes in for some criticism by the Jewish Sages who say:

• He was only righteous in comparison to the wickedness around him. (see Genesis 6:9)

• He didn't have the compassion to protest or care about others such as Abram did regarding the judgment on Sodom and Gomorrah.

• He should have been eager to leave the ark and start life all over again and not wait until God told him to. In Genesis 8:15 the word *'deber'* is used – a stronger way of speaking.

However, there are also many positive *midrashim*[5] about Noah including one that speaks of him warning others. As it does not say that he did in the Genesis account, it was probably this midrash that Peter was referring to in 2 Peter 2:5 when he calls him a 'preacher of righteousness'. This is one of several places in the New Testament when the 'Oral Law'[6] is quoted.

In Genesis 6:14, the covering of the ark was to be 'pitch' as it is usually translated. The word is *koper,* something that covers or protects. It comes from the same word that means 'atonement'. Atonement is also a covering and protection. It protects us from the wrath of God that we deserve for sin. The Hebrew word for ark, is *teva,* and that word is used only for Noah's ark and Moses' 'basket' in Exodus 2:3. *"But when she could no longer hide him, she took an ark of bulrushes for him, daubed it with asphalt and pitch, put the child in it, and laid* it *in the reeds by the river's bank."* This was also protected with pitch, or *koper,* by Moshe's (Moses) mother. In both cases, it was a divinely guided vessel.

## Genesis 7 & 8
## A New Beginning

In chapter 7:16, God ensures that Noah and his family are safely inside before He Himself shuts them in, something like a baby

---

[5] A simple explanation of Midrash is that it is commentary and can include stories to illustrate the meaning of a Biblical text.
[6] A very short explanation is that the Oral Law is a legal commentary on the Torah, explaining how the commandments should be carried out. (Jewish Virtual Library)

being tucked into bed by a loving parent. And so, the earth was immersed and cleansed in a giant *mikveh*[7].

In Genesis 8:20-21 the LORD smells a soothing aroma. We realise that God doesn't need to smell roast lamb, but a burnt offering means that the total animal is consumed on the altar. This is how Noah offered his thanks after leaving the ark. It expressed his dedication and worship of the LORD and it was this that pleased God's heart.

Something interesting in the narrative of Noah is pointed out by Rabbi Sacks[8], in one of his 'Covenant and Conversation' commentaries. Just as Adam and Chava learned from trying to blame others for their sin that there is such a thing as individual responsibility, and after killing his brother Kayin learned that there is a moral responsibility, so Noah, who by his obedience saved his family, learned collective responsibility.

## Genesis 9
## Justice and Love

The rainbow, the beautiful sign of God's mercy and promise, is comprised of seven colours. It was the guarantee that never again would there be such a flood, (verse11). The word covenant, in Hebrew - *brit* - is mentioned seven times between verses 8 and

---

[7] A *mikveh* is similar to a baptismal pool. A Jew immerses him or herself totally for a symbolic cleansing, for various religious occasions.
[8] Chief Rabbi of the United Hebrew Congregations in the UK from 1991 to 2013

17. Again, the number seven, a number that represents Divine perfection.

In this chapter, verses 20-23, we read of Noah's shame of becoming drunk and lying naked. Noah's humiliation was exposed by his youngest son, Ham. His brothers, Shem and Japheth/*Yafet*, covered their father's shame by draping a garment over him as they walked in backwards. *"And Shem and Japheth took a garment, and laid* it *upon both their shoulders, and went backward, and covered the nakedness of their father; and their faces* were *backward, and they saw not their father's nakedness."* And as Shem is mentioned first and the verb 'took'- is in the singular, it seems that it was he who initiated it. Therefore, say the Rabbis, it is his descendants to whom was given the honour of attaching tassels to their garments that spoke of the commandments. The tassels are to be on each of the four corners of a rectangle garment, and are knotted in a way that represents the 613 commandments in fulfilment of the biblical commandment in Numbers 15:37-39, *"Speak to the children of Israel: Tell them to make tassels on the corners of their garments throughout their generations, and to put a blue thread in the tassels of the corners."* Many of God's chosen people, the descendants of Shem, wear a daily visual reminder that they have been given the responsibility of living holy lives by obeying the commandments of God, because they are in covenant with a holy God.

The account of Noah's humiliation is another example of a principle established by God in this Book of Beginnings. We are not to expose or look on the shame or humiliation of others. In Matthew 1:19, Joseph set a wonderful example when he did not want to expose Mary to public disgrace because of her pregnancy. *"Then Joseph her husband, being a just man, and not wanting to make her a public example, was minded to put her away secretly."*

1 Peter 4:8 NIV says, *"...love covers over a multitude of sins."*

## Genesis 10
## The Families of the Earth

Be aware that genealogies are highly significant within Judaism. We will note a few things.

Although Shem is generally mentioned first, there is debate about who was the oldest of Noah's sons.

It is the descendants of Japeth/*Yafet* who begin the family tree. His name speaks of enlargement or space, a concept within the blessing he received from his father in 9:26. His descendants settled around the Black and Caspian Seas but later migrated north into Europe, and as 10:5 says, the people of the Coastlands came from them. The rest of Noah's blessing asks that Yafet will 'dwell in the tents of Shem'. The expression, dwelling in tents, can mean in Biblical understanding, to learn of God's word. Generally, today, the Gentile descendants of Yafet are from the families of the earth who have benefitted indeed from the Word of God, thanks to the descendants of Shem, from which came the family of Abraham.

Noah and Shem were both alive when Abraham was born. Noah died when Abraham was 58 years old (Genesis 9:28) and

Shem lived at least 600 years, (Genesis 11:11). Abraham may have heard the stories of pre and post Flood life from his (many greats) Grandfather Shem.

The modern names of the four nations that sprang from Ham, are Ethiopian, Egyptians, Libyans, and the collection of Biblical era tribes who collectively, are called the Canaanites.

## Genesis 11
## Relevant Judgement

It is incredibly interesting that in 11:5, God Himself 'comes down' to see the city and the tower which is being build. Radak[9] says that when God wishes to examine the deeds of lowly man, he 'descends' to observe the conditions among the sinners. Later in the Torah we see that a judge must not condemn until he meticulously examines the case. In Exodus 19:20 and Psalm 18:9, God again lowers Himself on Mt Sinai to elevate the People of Israel to the status of a chosen Nation. What a picture of the God of the universe coming down to man's level. Ephesians 4:10, *"He who descended is also the One who ascended far above all the heavens, that He might fill all things."*

Note that Jewish sages say that the generation of the Flood did not plan a rebellion against God as did the generation of Babel, (Genesis 11:4). The first punishment (the Flood) saw the world destroyed and the second, only dispersion and separation.

---

[9] Radak is an acronym for Rabbi David Kimchi from southern France, (1160 – 1235CE)

Rashi[10] said that therefore strife with each other is considered worse than rebellion against God. Strife between people in Jewish teaching is viewed as hateful. There are many verses in the New Testament that urges the new Gentile Believers to live in peace with each other. It is a pattern firmly laid down in the Torah.

It is significant that at the building of the tower of Babel, before language separated them, the people had a great degree of unity and worked together to '*make a name for themselves*' (11:4). In these days, through the explosion of knowledge and cooperation in trade and scientific endeavours, a global unity is developing and unfortunately again, not to glorify God, but man. This could bring about a situation such as described in Zechariah 14:2, "*For I will gather all the nations to battle against Jerusalem...*" At the end times, a global confederation could easily challenge God and His people.

In this chapter, we continue with the theme of dividing and separating, as the division of nations takes place through the dispersion (Genesis 11:9). In Jewish tradition the number of nations is 70, and this is derived from Deuteronomy 32:8, "*When the Most High divided their inheritance to the nations, When He separated the sons of Adam, He set the boundaries of the peoples according to the number of the children of Israel.*"

---

[10] Rabbi Shlomo Yitzhaki, (Hebrew: רבי שלמה יצחקי), better known by the acronym Rashi (February 22, 1040 – July 13, 1105), was a rabbi from France, famed as the author of the first comprehensive commentaries on the Talmud, Torah, and Tanakh (Hebrew Bible). (*Online New World Encyclopedia*).

And Genesis 46:27 tells us, that *"All the persons of the house of Jacob who went to Egypt were seventy."*

## Genesis 12
## The Sojourner

Then one nation was set apart. It began with Abram/*Avram*.

Leviticus 20:26, *"And you shall be holy to Me, for I the LORD am holy, and have separated you from the peoples, that you should be Mine…"*

1Kings 8:53, *"For You have separated them from all the peoples of the earth to be Your inheritance, as You spoke by our servant Moses, when You brought our fathers out of Egypt, O LORD God."*

The command that God gave to Avram in Genesis 12:1, was '*Lech l'chah*', literally meaning - 'go for yourself'. 'For yourself' or 'for your own sake' implies that obedience to God's leading, although it may be very difficult, is a blessing.

Avram left a place of security, and undertook a journey of insecurity, for an unknown destination. Hebrews 11:8 confirms this: *"By faith Abraham obeyed when he was called to go out to the place which he would receive as an inheritance. And he went out, not knowing where he was going."*

He is a role model for us – not only his strong faith in God, but a lifestyle that embodied:

17

- The pilgrim life. In Genesis 12:8, the mention of a tent speaks of a temporary life style. In the following verse, two verbs are used, translated as 'journeyed' and 'going on' in the NIV and others that indicate a dynamic, continuing travelling.

- The consecrated life. Also in Genesis 12:8, the mention of an altar speaks not only of worship of God but it was also a declaration that Avram's God was the Authority over that area. The belief at that time was that each area had its own god and when you went into another region, you came under the authority of its god. Avram was a bold witness to whatever community he lived in, that there was only one true God.

- Hospitality. This is demonstrated in Genesis 18:6-7, he hurried to wait on his guests.

- Compassion. Even though Sodom and Gomorrah, (Hebrew pronunciation - *S'dom* and *Amorrah)* were known for their wickedness, Abram tried to save the people from judgement, though he acknowledged God as the Judge of all the earth.

In Genesis 12:1-3 we again come across the number 'seven'. There are seven promises of God in these verses, just as there are seven branches of the menorah.

The seventh promise links the chosen nation to the Gentile nations. The famous Rabbi, Maimonides, also known as 'the

Rambam'[11], says the commandment to love God, includes taking the love of God to the entire world. Later, when God entered into covenant with the 'first Jew', the name Avram, which means a 'great father', became Abraham/*Avraham*, 'father of many nations'.

Within those three verses though is a warning as well as a promise. In 12:3, there are two different words for 'curse'. The cursing that can be done towards Abraham and his descendants is *mekalelcha*, the root of which also means to despise, to make light of. Whereas the cursing that God threatens, is a different word that means a strong form of cursing. The nations of the world, and even many Christian denominations, need to take heed. It is not just aggressive acts of hate against God's people that result in His judgement, but indifference, unjustified criticism and dislike.


## Genesis 13
## The Dividing and Separating Continues

Avram was told to leave his family but nephew Lot came with him. Following problems, Avram finally said in Genesis 13:9, *"Is not the whole land before you? Please separate yourself from me."* In 13:10 Lot 'saw' a well watered fertile area. Remember Eve who was guided by what she saw! His choice meant that he and his family would live amongst a perverted people,

---

[11] Maimonides was one of the most prolific and influential Torah scholars and physicians of the Middle Ages. He was born in Córdoba (present-day Spain).

which separated him not only geographically from Avram, but spiritually too.

God extended the blessing to Avram after the separation from family was complete. In 13:14, "The LORD said to Avram, after Lot had separated from him, *'Lift your eyes, and look from the place where you are'...*"

This is a good place to note the cost of discipleship. Yeshua said in Luke 14:26, *"If anyone comes to Me and does not hate his father and mother, wife and children, brothers and sisters, yes, and his own life also, he cannot be My disciple."* Remember that in accordance with the style of the Hebrew language, 'love' and 'hate' are juxtaposed to make a point. The Hebrew word *soneh* often translated 'hate' does not have the same meaning as in modern English. It is more to describe loving something or someone less, or in a different way, than the other.

Later, Ishmael is sent away from Isaac/*Yitzak* and the 'separating' continues in Genesis 36:6 when Esau/*Esaf*, the ungodly brother, separated himself from the presence of Jacob/*Yakov* and goes away to Edom.

## Genesis 14
## Messiah's Forerunner

In verse 18 we are introduced to the mysterious personage of *Melkhi-Tzedek*, whose name, or title, means King of Righteousness. He was not only a king but is also called a priest and his priesthood is mentioned in Psalm 110:4. An interesting point is that Melkhi-Tzedek, king of a Gentile city, was a Gentile who worshipped the LORD.

Psalm 110 is quoted in Hebrews 5:6 where it is explained that our king/priest/Messiah, who is from the line of Judah which is not the priestly tribe, will be made a priest after the order of Melkhi-Tzedek. A Jewish tradition identifies Melkhi-Tzedek as Shem who would have been still alive at the time of Avraham. (Genesis 11:10-26).

## Genesis 15-17
## The Abrahamic Covenant Extended

In 15:9-21 God reaffirmed His covenant with Avram and extended the blessing to include the promise of a land which was not included in the covenant promises made in 12:1-3. God used customs of the day to ratify the covenant known in Jewish commentary as the Covenant of the Halves. The animals which God told Avram to sacrifice in the ritual were the animals that would be used in the sacrifices as specified by the Torah. God's presence, symbolized by the smoking furnace and torch of fire, was with Avram during this intense experience. We see in Scripture that most commonly fire, or some form of it, indicated the Presence of the LORD.

Unfortunately, in chapter 16 we see Abram and Sarai take matters into their own hands and as can happen when we do that, they unwittingly initiated a problem that would bring distress to their people in later generations. Rejected Hagar flees the envy of Sarai and is found by the LORD at a well. The incident is reminiscent of the Samaritan woman, also rejected, also found at a well, by Messiah, as recorded in John's Gospel chapter 4.

In chapter 17 the covenant is again confirmed including the promise of land. Avram's name is changed to Abraham/*Avraham*, 'father of a multitude' and Sarai 'my princess' becomes Sarah 'princess to all'.

Now another commandment is added, that of circumcision. The significance of this Divine instruction will be dealt with in the following study, *'The Elegance of Exodus'*. What is important here though is the fact that God gave it to His Chosen People as a sign of the Covenant He had made with them through Avraham.

## Genesis 18
## Godly Characteristics

The opening verses of chapter 18 are considered by the Jewish sages to be an indication of an outstanding trait of Avraham— that of hospitality. He runs to meet his guests and immediately invites them to accept shelter and refreshment. In verse 6 he 'hurries', in verse 7, he 'ran' and 'hastened', so eager was he say the Rabbis, to be hospitable. Hospitality became a strong practice within Judaism and the new Gentile Believers were encouraged to follow the same ideal. "*...distributing to the needs of the saints, given to hospitality*" says Romans 12:13 and the NLT paraphrases 1 Peter 4:9 which tells us to "*Cheerfully* *share your home with those who need a meal or a place to stay."*

Although we do not hear of Avraham's immediate response to the glad news of a child the following year, it is not recorded anywhere that he doubted this seemingly impossible event. And if it seemed unfair that Sarah received a rebuke for her laughter, it was because while open laughter is a sign of joy, she laughed inwardly at the thought of something so unbelievable. The LORD who knows our thoughts, knew of her immediate doubt. But Hebrews 11:11 tells us of her restored faith, *"By faith Sarah herself also received strength to conceive seed, and she bore a child when she was past the age, because she judged Him faithful who had promised."*

In Genesis 18:21 we again see that God as the righteous judge uses the term to 'go down, descend' to see the sin of S'dom and Amorah. Avraham's reaction to the forthcoming destruction of Sodom and Gomorrah is one of compassion and he puts forth a case for God's mercy.

## Genesis 19
## Consequences of Choices

Sadly, there weren't even ten righteous (18:32), and so God's judgement came to bear. However, He showed mercy to Lot and his family by sending angels to warn them. The Hebrew for 'angel' is literally 'messenger' and can mean a human messenger. This case is interesting because they were the same messengers who had visited Avraham and he saw them as men. Lot though, saw them as angels, in verse 1. They had to force Lot's family to leave and even then, Lot's wife looked back in disobedience to what she had been instructed and so she perished. Lot was now paying the price for an easy but wrong choice of lifestyle. The cost was continued by the actions of his daughters which we assume would have been humiliating and degrading.

## Genesis 20
## Imperfect Vessels

In this chapter, and back in chapter 12:10-20, we are reminded that God's chosen vessels acted in ways that we find hard to understand. We need to remember that culture and the society in which they lived, especially Avraham's situation as a stranger in the region to which God had sent him, dictated norms of behaviour with which we are not familiar. Also note that the Bible does not whitewash the failures and lapses of our 'heroes'. Despite weaknesses, God forgives and uses those who are committed to His service.

In verse 17 is the first prayer for healing in the Bible, and it is for a pagan king. Avraham prayed for healing for Abimelech's household and God answered.

# Genesis 21
## Child of Promise

In verses 1–7 the child of promise is born and called Isaac/ *Yitzak*. The name means 'laughter' and now, no doubt, Sarah laughed with joy.

However, trouble comes to Avraham's household as Sarah demands that Hagar and her son be sent away. She may have had reason to be concerned about the elder boy's influence. The Hebrew word, *tsachaq*, is translated as 'scoffing or mocking' in verse 9. Jewish scholars say that the same verb is used in connection with idolatry in Exodus 32:6 in the incident of the Golden Calf, with adultery in Genesis 39:17 in the case of Potiphar's wife's accusations, and murder in 2nd Samuel 2:14. Therefore, what sounds like spiteful teasing may have been more troublesome behaviour, leading to Sarah's concern.

# Genesis 22
## Child of Sacrifice

While looking at the 'Binding of Yitzak' as this Biblical account is called in Jewish teaching, we can note two points. One is that in verse 2, the structure of the Hebrew indicates that God asked Abraham. It was not a usual command. A good reminder that God asks for our obedience. His commandments are not in the sense that a dictator commands obedience, but in the way a Father looks for respect and obedience from his children. The other point, is that the Jewish people make a connection from the 'binding of Yitzak' to the *tefilin*[12] which is bound each morning on the head and arms of the observant Jewish man in obedience to Exodus 13:9. The *tefilin* are to remind them of God's commandments and their obedience to them. As they are wrapped/bound to the head and arm, they represent both intellect and actions, both of which ought to be employed in the walk of obedience to the commandments throughout the day.

As father and son walked to the place of sacrifice, his son bore the wood that would provide the sacrificial fire, a powerful picture of John 19:17, where another begotten son would bear the wood that facilitated His sacrifice. Both sons were under the authority of the Father. *"And He, bearing His cross, went out to a place called the Place of a Skull, which is called in Hebrew, Golgotha."*

The ram caught in a thicket of thorns, Genesis 22:13, is an embedded picture that needs no explaining. The substitute sacrifice!

In Genesis 22:18, again the nations are included in the blessing of Avraham. As a result of his total dedication and trust, demonstrated by his willingness to sacrifice his 'only' (the Hebrew is *yachid* meaning *unique*) son, the blessing that followed was given by God to Avraham with a strong binding oath (Genesis 22:16). This is indicated by the word, *shava*, a strong form of an oath.

---

[12] Tefilin are a set of small black leather boxes containing scrolls of parchment inscribed with verses from the Torah.

The word *shava* is from the same root as the word for 'seven'. Not only is 'seven' linked to 'Divine perfection' but it was considered a powerful unbreakable number as it could not be divided by small numbers. Back in Genesis chapter 21 is the story of the oath that was made between Abimelech and Avraham. It was sealed with the gift of seven lambs and the place where the exchange took place was Beersheeba, literally, 'Well of the Seven'.

## Genesis 23
## Purchase of Land in the Promised Land

In chapter 23 some typical Middle Eastern bargaining takes place. Finally, the first legal purchase of land takes place in Hebron, the location where God would (in 2 Samuel 2:1) direct David to take up residence. This is also where he would be anointed King and from Hebron reign for seven and a half years before he conquered the Jebusite city, Jerusalem.

'*Israel 365*', an Israel based information service, points out in one of their daily emails, that the name Hebron/*Chevron* has profound significance. The Hebrew name Chevron is a contraction of the word *chaver*, 'friend', and the word *na'eh*, 'beloved'. The very name of the city of Chevron alludes to its most famous resident Avraham, who was the first beloved friend of the LORD, as is written in Isaiah 41:8, "*Seed of Avraham, My friend.*"

Another ancient legal purchase in the Promised Land was made by Yakov as recorded in Joshua 24:32, "*The bones of Joseph, which the children of Israel had brought up out of Egypt, they buried at Shechem, in the plot of ground which Jacob had bought from the sons of Hamor the father of Shechem for one hundred pieces of silver, and which had become an inheritance of the children of Joseph."*

And in Jerusalem, David buys the threshing floor of Araunah (2 Samuel 24:21-24), which eventually becomes the site of the Temple and today is known as the Temple Mount.

It is interesting that these three places, Hebron, Shechem and the Temple Mount in Jerusalem, are three hotly contested areas today.

## Genesis 24
### Seeking out the Bride

The Father sends a trusted servant to find a bride for the Son. The guidance was unerring, and the servant was led to the right person. A point of interest is verse 15 which mentions that Rebecca/*Rivka* was carrying a pitcher on her shoulder. It shows the exactness of the Bible, even in small things. For the women in Mesopotamia, as well as Syria (Aram), carried their water jar this way on their shoulder, while in Israel, then Canaan, and most other parts of the Middle East, the jar was balanced on the head.

In verse 57 we see that the girl had to be willing to become the bride. She was not forced against her will. It is because of this example that Judaism insists that in arranged marriages, the girl is not without choice in the matter. It is also of course, part of the picture that Jewish marriages give us, of Messiah and the Bride he seeks. There is no forcing of will.

## Genesis 25
### The Separating Continues

Although Abraham took another wife, her sons were sent eastward, just as Ishmael had been sent away.

In verse 11, following the death of Abraham, God blesses Yitzak, thus confirming that he is the rightful son in the eyes of God. In verse 21, like Sarah and Abraham, God's supernatural intervention was needed to ensure that the chosen line, the line of Messiah - whose conception was also supernatural - would continue. In fact, this Divine intervention is required in the case of each matriarch. Even Leah who would bear seven children, must have been barren, just as her sister Rachel was. In Genesis 29:31 we read, *"When the LORD saw that Leah was unloved, he opened up her womb."* If she had not been barren, there would have been no need for a supernatural 'opening of the womb'.

## Genesis 26
### Prophetic Wells

A global pattern is set, sadly, in verse 14. Yitzak prospered and the other citizens of the land (in this case the Philistines) became jealous. Jealousy and suspicion of Jews has often resulted in anti-Semitism, which in turn has led to expulsion, and/or, terrible persecution. It was jealousy and suspicion that Hitler played on, ending in a horror that was witnessed but not generally protested, by their fellow citizens.

Yitzak named each well that described the situation he faced. The first in verse 20 was *Esek* which meant 'quarrel', then *Sitnah* meaning 'hatred', and finally *Rehovot* meaning 'open and wide'. Even through difficult times, God's promises of fruitfulness still stand. He brings His servants through times of testing to seasons of blessing.

## Genesis 27 & 28
## God's Choices

Like the story of Noah, the Christian perception of Jacob/ *Yakov* we read in Genesis 25:26-28:4, differs from the Jewish one. Usually in Christian teaching, the emphasis is on 'Jacob the Deceiver', but a softer picture is painted when the text is explored. Yakov is described in English as a mild man, in Genesis 25:27. But that is translated from *'tam'* which means, 'unblemished'. It is the same word that is applied to the sacrifices – they had to be unblemished/*tam*. A hunter in Jewish thought, has negative connotations, while someone 'dwelling in tents', implies that they were studiers of God's word. Esau/*Esaf* seemed to live for the moment and possibly killed for pleasure; after all, where was the game and why was he hungry in 25:29-34 when he carelessly traded his birthright for food?

While there are a lot of details and depth to this story, we will skip over to the so-called deception and note a few things from the drama.

Firstly, Rivka knew the prophetic statements about her younger twin son (Genesis 25:23). Secondly, there was hesitancy on the part of Yakov. From the Hebrew text we know that he approached his father with politeness, (Genesis 27:18) unlike Esaf's character, giving his father reason to be suspicious. Thirdly, Yitzak did not actually pass on the Abrahamic blessing while he thought it **was** Esaf, showing that he also knew the character of his firstborn. Genesis 25:28 is speaking perhaps, of a conditional love! That important Abrahamic blessing was bestowed later upon Yakov when he was leaving for Padan Aram.

Lastly, a very poignant and thought provoking question was asked by Yakov. One we need to ask sometimes. Genesis 27:12, *"Perhaps my Father will feel me, and I shall seem to be a deceiver?"* Psalms 51 and 139 are good starting points as we ask God to examine our inner lives.

The 'brave' hunter might have seemed to us a better choice than a 'homebody' but God knows the hearts and does His own choosing. His choice is confirmed dramatically in Malachi 1:2-3 and Romans 9:13. Refer back to Genesis chapter 13 of this Study, to see how 'love' and 'hate' are juxtaposed to make a point.

We know though that Yakov had much to learn, and later was on the receiving end of deception when his Uncle Laban substituted Leah for his beloved Rachel. It imitated his deception of Yitzak. Much later he abhorred his sons' deception of Hamor and Shekhem as seen in Genesis 34:30 and 49:5.

In chapter 28 Yakov leaves his family. His mother, who had encouraged him to deceive his father, would never see her favoured son again. He arrived at a place which, after his amazing dream, he named Bethel/*Bet El*, the House of God. It is thought by Jewish scholars that this was in fact Mt. Moriah, the place that the temple would one day stand. Verse 22 seems to bear this out. In his dream the LORD Himself blesses him with the blessing of Abraham and yet in spite of all that happens he still makes a pact with God to really have proof that God is with him. Verse 20-21, *"If God is with me...so that I come back to my Father's house in peace, then shall the LORD be my God."* And it will not be until he has an encounter in Genesis 32:30 that he can say, *"I have seen God face to face."*

### Genesis 29 & 30
### The Rejected Wife

Leah's desperation to be loved as much as Rachel, tears at our heartstrings because many of us know the feeling of being shut out – of someone's life, or a circle, or a family. Rejection is a common and soul-destroying emotion. Proverbs 18:14 KJV asks *"...a wounded spirit who can bear?"* Some people tragically know rejection all their lives from many sources, for others it may be from one source only, but still painful. However, as in the case of Hagar, who was also a rejected wife, God sees! Even if nobody else does! (Genesis 29:31 and chapter 16:13).

Leah could not have foreseen the role God had for her. It was she after all who was an ancestress of the Messiah! She bore Judah, 29:35, and it was from the line of Judah that Messiah would come.

King David was of the tribe of Judah, and a descendant of his as God promised in many scriptures, would be the Anointed One, the Messiah. Isaiah 9:7, "*Of the increase of His government and peace there will be no end, upon <u>the throne of David</u> and over His kingdom…*" and Isaiah 16:5, "*In mercy the throne will be established; And One will sit on it in truth, in <u>the tabernacle of David</u>, Judging and seeking justice and hastening righteousness.*" Yeshua's genealogy in Matthew 1:1 begins, "*The book of the genealogy of Jesus Christ, <u>the Son of David</u>, the Son of Abraham.*"

## Genesis 31-33
## Again, Separation

In 31:3, The LORD knew it was time for Yakov 'to seek the shelter of Israel', as expressed by the Chofetz Chayim[13].

The attitude of Laban and his sons grew dark. No matter what Laban did to hinder Yakov economically, God prospered him.

---

[13] Israel Meir Kagan (1838-1933), Talmudic and rabbinic scholar, ethical and religious teacher, and usually referred to as Chofetz Chayyim, is venerated for his saintliness and learning. (My Jewish Learning)

As happened in the later history of the Jewish people, jealousy leading to terrible persecution, has often pushed the Jews back to their Promised Land from their scattered exile.

Now Yakov had to face his fear, which was a consequence of his actions concerning his brother. He prepared his story and his placations and sent out spies, but in 32:6 it seemed Esaf also had spies and knew about his pending arrival. In 32:9-12, Yakov prayed, reminding God of His promises - a good pattern for a prayer of petition. God says later in Isaiah 43:26 when desiring to extend mercy and forgiveness towards sinful Israel, *"Put Me in remembrance; Let us contend together; State your case, that you may be acquitted."*

The strange wrestling match which invites various Jewish and Christian explanations, transforms Yakov, whose name is derived from 'deceitful', into 'Israel'. This can mean 'one who struggles with God', or 'one for whom God fights'. The first three Hebrew letters of the name *Isr*-ael can be read as *yeshar,* meaning straight or honest, which is the opposite to his name Yakov, which had the connotation of deceitful or dishonest. David Nekrutman[14] points out that the name could also come from the Hebrew letters in 'I-*sra*-el'- that say, *'serara'/* authority. I-*sr*-a-*el* can also mean, 'prince/*sar* of God/*El'*.

It is interesting to note, that out of the three patriarchs, God links his name and identity to imperfect Yakov more than the others, such as one of many references, Psalm 114:7. *"Tremble, O earth, at the presence of the Lord, At the presence of the*

---

[14] Executive Director for the Centre for Jewish-Christian Understanding and Cooperation in Jerusalem.

<u>*God of Jacob*</u>." What an encouragement for us. In spite of our failures, God is not ashamed of us. We should not be ashamed of Him.

So Yakov is in the Promised Land and Esaf, (in 33:16), goes east, away from it. Genesis 36:6 confirms the separation.

## Genesis 34 & 35
## When Things Go Wrong

In chapter 34 we see a sordid tale of deceit and bloodshed. Shekhem protests love for Dina but he had violated her. Yakov is seemingly passive, perhaps working out what to do in face of a strong tribe in his new land. Two brothers react with violence. No one comes out clean, even Dina, whom Jewish commentators rebuke for her careless unaccompanied wandering. We should also note something else, that there may be a hint of more than innocent love from a prince. The brothers hatch a plan to rescue her and tell Shekhem and his father that if they agree to circumcision, they can exchange daughters in marriage. However, Hamor and Shekhem relate more than that to their people. In 34:23 they add, "*will not their livestock, their property, and every animal of theirs be ours?*" They were possibly seeing an opportunity for plunder and gain.

It is to be noted too, that in 49:5-7 when Yakov delivers his prophetic blessings to his sons before his death, he stated in what was more like a curse, "*Simeon and Levi* are *brothers; instruments of cruelty are in their dwelling place...I will divide them in Jacob, and scatter them in Israel.*" The tribe of Simeon was small and never amounted to anything significant. Their allotted portion and the tribe were absorbed by the large tribe of Judah. The tribe of Levi while set aside as the priestly nation due to their stand against idolatry in the wilderness journey, were distributed across Israel and never inherited a tribal portion.

God moves Yakov on, back to where his spiritual journey started, the place he named Bet El, the House of God. It's good to remember our starting point with God in our life, when things get out of our control. It must be noted though that in preparation, Yakov in Genesis 35:2-4, ensured his household was freed from idolatrous influences that hinder fellowship with the God of Israel. It was at Bet El in 35:11-12 that God confirms with Yakov, the Abrahamic covenant. In the English, God calls Himself *El Shaddai* which is usually translated as 'God Almighty' but that is not an accurate translation. El Shaddai does have the connotation of God's sovereignty but not as in power. The Hebrew word *shad* means breast from which it is believed *Shaddai* (lit. 'my breast') is derived. Therefore, the name has the meaning of nourishment, sustenance, provision and parental love. The All Sufficient One is more accurate. There are different opinions from scholars about the full meaning of the word.

The tragic death of Yakov's beloved wife, Rachel, was probably due in part to a breech birth as 35:17 indicates. Even before the baby was born, the midwife proclaimed it a son, therefore she could obviously see his genitals.

With her last breaths, Rachel names her son *Ben Oni* – 'son of my sorrow'. Yakov though, renames him *Ben Yamin* (Benjamin) which means 'son of the right' signifying direction, that is to the right of east, south. In Jewish thought east is the principal point of the compass. Therefore, his name can mean 'son of the south', emphasising that he was born south of Padan Aram where Yakov had been in a kind of exile for so long. Benyamin was the only son to be born in the Promised Land, (Canaan at that stage). His name can also be taken to mean 'son of strength', as the right hand represents strength and power. We can find some parallels here with Messiah who was called 'A Man of Sorrows' and sits at the Father's right hand. *"...sat down at the right hand of the throne of God."* Hebrews 12:2. Many scriptures too speak the Right Hand of God as the instrument of His power and sovereignty.

In Genesis 35, verse 21 is significant because for the first time, *migdal eder,* which means 'tower of the flock', was mentioned. This is the area in which the shepherds were guarding their flock when they heard the good news of Messiah's birth.

This area on the outskirts of Bethlehem is also mentioned in the Talmudic[15] writings which state that all livestock surrounding Jerusalem as far as migdal eder, were deemed to be holy and could only be used for sacrifices in the Temple. The shepherds in the fields of Bethlehem were guarding sacrificial flocks.

Micah 4:8 also refers to migdal eder. *"And you, O tower of the flock, the stronghold of the daughter of Zion, to you shall it*

---

[15] A very short explanation is that the Talmud, also known as the Oral Law is a legal commentary on the Torah, explaining how the commandments should be carried out. (Jewish Virtual Library)

*come, even the former dominion shall come, the kingdom of the daughter of Jerusalem."*

Based on that prophecy, prominent Jewish writers concluded that it would be at migdal eder where the arrival of the Messiah would be declared first.

Now that we have been introduced to all the patriachs and matriachs of the tribes of Israel we can take note of something interesting. The first Hebrew letter of each of their names are the same letters that spell the word Israel. ישראל . The first letter 'yud' begins the names of Yitzak and Yakov; the second letter 'sheen', is the first letter of Sarah; the third is 'resh', the beginning of Rivka and Rachel; the fourth is 'aleph', the first letter of Avraham; the last letter is 'lamed' which is the first letter of Leah. The seven names (seven again!) use a total of 12 different letters – the number of tribes which came from them. Also, the total number of letters used to spell the seven names, comes to 26 which is the numerical value of the *'yud heh vav heh'* Name of God.

## Genesis 36 & 38
## Family Aberrations

Genesis 36 is one of those inserted chapters of the Torah, not necessarily fitting any chronological time frame but supplying context or background. In this case it is the genealogy of Esav. We will note a few things only.

This passage makes it clear that Esav is Edom and that he was the father of the Edomic Kingdom. Their territory was in what is called Jordan today, located south of Moab. The Israelites considered them kinsmen and we will come across some interaction later although it is not positive. During the time of the Maccabees[16] who conquered the area of Edom, there were many forced conversions to Judaism. Herod the Great was an Edomite, or in Greek, Idumean.

There was one clan that sprang from Esav not considered kin at all. This clan was the Amalekites, descendants from Amalek the son of Esav's son and his son's concubine, 35:12. The Amalekites became bitter enemies of the people of God of whom we will learn more later.

Another point of interest is that Job lived in the Land of Uz which was part of Edom. (Job 1:1).

Psalm 137:7 NIV is one of several scriptures which indicate their ongoing resentment against their Jewish 'cousins'. *"Remember, LORD, what the Edomites did on the day Jerusalem fell. 'Tear it down,' they cried, 'tear it down to its foundations'!"* In the Jewish mind, Edom has come to represent an anti-Semitic spirit, particularly, sadly, as found in Western Christendom.

---

[16] The Maccabees, also spelled Machabees, were a group of Jewish rebel warriors who took control of Judea, which at the time was part of the Seleucid Empire. They founded the Hasmonean dynasty, which ruled from 167 BCE to 37 BCE, being a fully independent kingdom from about 110 to 63 BCE. Wikipedia

We will look now at chapter 38 to see what God has embedded in this account for us. We first see in 38:1 that Judah/*Yehudah* departed from his brothers. Leaving your 'brothers' is a move that like Yehudah's decision, can lead to wrong alliances, wrong decisions and wrong consequences. He was not supposed to marry a Canaanite woman. His uncle Esaf had done that, bringing pain to Rivka and Yitzak, Genesis 28:8.

Although this chapter looks like a tale of immorality, the Torah does not present it as that and the Jewish sages praise Tamar for doing what is right by the Torah. Yehudah's second son should have provided a son for his dead brother as was the custom of that day and common in various cultures and later became enshrined in the 'Mosaic Law'. After that son's death, Yehudah should have given his third son to Tamar who, because she could see that was not going to happen, took matters into her own hands. We know she did the right thing because she was rewarded by being in the messianic line. Tamar, the Rabbis tell us was Semitic, and so her union with Yehudah ensured that Canaanite blood did not come through Yehudah's wrong choice of partner. In spite of the unrighteous behaviour of all concerned, God went to great lengths to ensure the covenantal bloodline would be protected.

A good time to look at what we could call an unsavoury family tree of our Messiah and be reminded that God is above our mistakes and failures and also does not work according to our own ideas of how things should be and people should act. Those in the Messianic line also includes Rahab, a prostitute; Ruth, a descendant of Moab, the nation from Lot and his daughter;

David and Bathsheba's line whose marriage was only after an adulterous relationship.

## Genesis 37 & 39-50
## Joseph – the 'Gentilized' Deliverer

These chapters tell the fascinating and dramatic story of Joseph/ *Yosef.* The story reminds us of the Book of Esther when God's Unseen Hand directs events to bring about deliverance for the Jewish people, placing an unlikely person in a position of influence. An example of someone who 'just happened to be' there at the right time in Yosef's story is in 37:15-17, when an unnamed man - or angel? - could direct Yosef to his brothers. And from there, situations unfold to get the chosen family into Egypt where God intended them to be where he could refine and test them in the furnace of Egypt. *"But the LORD has taken you and brought you out of the iron furnace, out of Egypt, to be His people, an inheritance, as you are this day."* Deuteronomy 4:20. The LORD uses seemingly trivial happenings as well as major ones on behalf of His people.

Deceit again touched Yakov when his sons brought him the coat that marked Yosef as the favoured son. Such a coat was fit for the children of kings as we learn in 2 Samuel 13:18, *"Now she had on a robe of many colors, for the king's virgin daughters wore such apparel."* They had dipped the coat in the blood of a kid goat, just as he had used a kid goat to deceive his father. (Genesis 27:16).

Another robe belonging to a King will also be 'dipped in blood' as we read in the dramatic 19ᵗʰ chapter of Revelation, verse 13.

This is one of the many connections between Yosef and Yeshua.

It is interesting to note one of the several traditions in Jewish teaching about the Messiah, is that there will be two messiahs one day, Messiah Son of Joseph and Messiah Son of David. According to tradition, the Messiah Son of Joseph will unite all Israel in preparation for the arrival of the Messiah Son of David but will die in the process in an act of self-sacrifice for his people.

Yosef was the eventual deliverer of Israel. Firstly though, he was betrayed, left for dead, then elevated to a high position and eventually held the life and death of the people in his hands. Before his brothers recognised him, he first reigned and saved Gentiles.

In this story, there is much from which we can learn and benefit, and all the way through, the parallels to Yeshua make a detailed study on its own. I want to point out one important point.

Teaching regarding the person of the Messiah within Judaism is not as black and white and clear cut as Christian teaching and interpretation. Christians sometimes ask why the Jews cannot recognise Yeshua in the Scriptures. Here is one good reason.

When Yosef's brothers went to Egypt, they did not recognise him! Yosef was dressed like a Gentile and spoke like a Gentile. This is what Christianity has done to Yeshua. His brothers, the Jewish people, don't recognise him. We have taken Him and his teaching away from His Jewish setting. Over the centuries, we have tragically acted towards His brothers in an unbelievably cruel and hateful way so it looks impossible to Jews that He could be their deliverer. Thankfully, many Gentile Believers are realising this shame and like Ruth, are coming from a despised people (in our case meaning those who have been the persecutors of Jews) to humbly take hold of the corner of the garment of a Jew (Zechariah 8:23).

The Hebrew word for corner, *kanaf*, is also translated as 'wings'. It is also the word for the corner of the garment from which the tassels hang, as commanded by God in Numbers 15:38. The tassels – called *tzitzit* – represent both the commandments of God and the wings of protection which God provides, in the same way that a bird's wings protect her young.

We Gentiles, like Ruth, have come under the wings of protection of the God of Israel, just as Boaz expressed in Ruth 2:12 when he blessed Ruth with these words, *"The LORD repay your work, and a full reward be given you by the LORD God of Israel, under whose wings you have come for refuge."*

May we delight in that relationship and learn to delight ourselves in the Torah as the Jewish people have for thousands of years.

Blessed is the man who walks not in the counsel of the ungodly....but his delight is in the Torah of the LORD and in His Torah he meditates day and night. Psalm 1:1,2

# THE ELEGANCE OF EXODUS

As we continue to glean in the 'fields of Boaz', may we see the delight of the Torah, those divine instructions given to a set-apart people so they would represent a holy God by living holy lives.

'Elegance', is certainly a word that can be used as a theme throughout this Book. The descendants of Abraham had become slaves, and from this lowly social class, were <u>elevated</u> to a priestly nation status. They were called by the God of the Universe, My *'Segula'*, My (private) Treasure. The Rabbis say that while slaves, they had reached the lowest level of impurity and were in danger of going beyond redemption. In Ezekiel 20:6-7 God said, *"On that day I raised My hand in an oath to them, to bring them out of the land of Egypt into a land that I had searched out for them, flowing with milk and honey, the glory of all lands. Then I said to them, 'Each of you, throw away the abominations which are before his eyes, and do not defile yourselves with the idols of Egypt. I am the LORD your God',"* and again in Ezekiel 23:3, God refers to their sinful state while in Egypt, when he is speaking of the sin of Judah and Samaria in Ezekiel's time. *"They committed harlotry in Egypt, they committed harlotry in their youth."*

# Exodus 1 & 2
## Redemption at Hand

The Hebrew name of Exodus is *Shmot* which means 'names' because the Book begins with the names of the male descendants of Jacob/*Yakov* who came to Egypt. As mentioned in 'Gems from Genesis', the number of nations was according to the Children of Israel, and both Exodus 1:5 and Deuteronomy 32:8 tell us that the number of Yakov's family when they went into Egypt, was seventy in all.

The Ramban[17] says that the Book of Exodus is the Book of Redemption, and we see that God is beginning to put his plan of redemption, of deliverance, into action.

In 1:8-10 the age old fear of 'the Jew being different' and jealousy of their prosperity raises its head here and so measures are ordered to place Joseph/*Yosef's* family in subjugation. Later harsher measures come into play and we see the beginning of genocide.

Brave midwives, 1:17, defied the Pharaoh's orders to kill baby boys in what may be the first example of civil disobedience in order to uphold the higher law of God. In 2:3, Moses/*Moshe* was placed into the Nile as Pharaoh ordered, but, under the protection of God in a vessel which is called for the second and last time in the Bible in Hebrew, a *teva* - the same name as the ark of Noah.

---

[17] Nahmanides, also known as Rabbi Moses ben Naḥman Girond and by his acronym Ramban, was a leading medieval Jewish scholar, born in Spain.

Let us note something significant about Moses's name. It is Egyptian, (*Meses*) and given to him by an Egyptian, the Pharaoh's daughter. Remember, that it is God Himself who changed the names of Abram and Sarai to Abraham and Sarah, names their son Isaac and changes Jacob's name to Israel. Even though Joseph had been given an Egyptian name, it is Joseph by which we remember him. Moses may have had a Hebrew name given to him by his parents, but it is the name given to him by his adoptive Egyptian mother who saved his life, that this great prophet and deliverer is known by. The reason, says a midrash,[18] is that:

'This is the reward for those who do kindness. Although Moses had many names, the only one by which he is known in the whole Torah is the one given to him by the daughter of Pharaoh. Even the Holy One, blessed be He, did not call him by any other name'.

After Moshe's privileged upbringing, we see him in his first appearance of 'redeemer' when he saves one of his Hebrew brothers from violence, perhaps death. However, although a love for his people is clear from the start, in 2:14 his role as redeemer is rejected by other slaves. Knowing his killing the Egyptian would bring a death sentence from Pharaoh, he flees to Midian. There, Moshe's compassion is demonstrated again when in 2:16-17 he helps seven daughters to water their flocks.

It can be noted that Midian was not a nation but a compilation of several tribes which had no political ties with Egypt. One of

---

[18] A very simple explanation of Midrash is that it is commentary and can include stories to illustrate the meaning of a Biblical text

the sons born to Abraham's second wife Keturah, was Midian (Genesis 25:2).

From Prince of Egypt to a lowly shepherd! Moshe accepted his new status with a determination and willingness to begin a new life as the Hebrew word *ya'al,* translated as 'was content', 2:21, indicates. The naming of his first son though, hints at a feeling of disconnection from the people to whom he truly belongs. *Gershom,* 2:22 is derived from the word for foreigner or stranger.

**Exodus 3 & 4**
**Gods Calling**

When Moshe is given his commission by God in chapter 3 to be the deliverer of his people, he is reluctant as many other prophets have been since. Moshe asks for His name. This is because, explains Tom Bradford, (www.torahclass.com):

'One of the main tenets of the Egyptian religion was that if you knew a particular god's name (and they had MANY gods) you could manipulate that god to do YOUR will by invoking his name. You see, just like in Hebrew, in the Egyptian language personal names held meanings. So, the name of a god denoted that god's characteristics, and that characteristic was directly associated to some specific part of the natural or spiritual world that he, or she, had control or influence over. God obliged and gave Moses a name: a name that denoted God's characteristics, and that name was **ehyeh asher ehyeh**'.

This name is usually translated as 'I am who I am' in English Bibles but, can be 'I will be who I will be' and in Judaism that is how it is usually understood.

In 3:16, God told Moshe to tell the elders of Israel that He has 'surely remembered them'. The sentence in Hebrew is '*Pakod Pakadeti Etchem*' and is possibly translated as 'visited' in your translation. In 4:29-31, Aaron conveys everything that the LORD had told Moshe and the people believed and worshipped. Why did they believe? It was because they recognised key words. Back in Genesis 50:24-26, before he died, Yosef said twice, "*...God will surely remember/paked you...*" There are other words that translate as 'remember', but *pakod* is used 37 times throughout the Hebrew Bible and this kind of remembering is to take heed of; to ensure all or everyone is accounted for; to act on behalf of.

In Exodus 6:1-8 when He reiterates His promise of deliverance in spite of worsening circumstances, He gives Moshe His personal name, YHVH, the transliterated letters being *yud-heh-vav-heh*. The Name is never pronounced by Jews today as the proper pronunciation has been lost. It is substituted with the name *Adona*i in prayer, or in everyday speech, *HaShem*, literally -The Name. In English translations, the four-letter Name of God is usually shown as LORD, the upper case letters distinguish it from 'Lord' which means master.

## God's Standards

Returning to Exodus 4:1, Moshe begins to voice his concerns and he is given signs to demonstrate that he comes to the people in the Name of the God of their forefathers. For the first time in Scripture, God gives a man the power to perform miracles.

In 4:1-8 God gives Moshe signs with which he could convince the people and that he truly had a message from God. His shepherd's rod became a snake, a symbol of impurity and then, when his hand touched the area of his heart, it was afflicted with *tza'arat*[19]. Both were symbols of impurity. The snake, or serpent, was also a symbol of Pharaoh's authority which, we later see, is decidedly overruled.

Note, in 4:13-16 after various excuses why he should not be the one to go to Pharaoh, Moshe finally begs God to find someone else, thus provoking God's anger. However, God knew his heart and reactions already, as he knows ours, and assures him that his brother Aaron has already been prepared and is on his way to meet him.

In Exodus 4:24-25 we learn how God sets a pattern for someone called to serve Him. That person's life needs to match up to His standards. Even Moshe it seems, had disobeyed the commandment of circumcision, a commandment already given to Abraham for all his descendants. It is good to note here that the Hebrew word *mila*/circumcision is not a word that means 'to cut', but 'to restrain, restrict'. Because it is to do with the male organ, circumcision symbolises restricting desires to within God's boundaries, His framework of holy living. That is why an uncircumcised heart is the symbol of a life lived without restraints, or in rebellion.

---

[19] Tzaarat is often translated as leprosy but this is not correct as the symptoms are not the same. The Rabbis understand it to be a spiritual condition that is usually connected to the sin of slander, or wrong speaking.

## Exodus 5-7
## God's Test of Faith

The reunited brothers go back to Egypt, a centre of idol worship. Later in Deuteronomy 4:20, Moshe would refer to Egypt as 'an iron furnace'. Pharaoh was considered a god and he had no time for another 'god' whose name he did not know.

Their efforts on behalf of their people only make matters worse for them, until Moshe cries in despair to the LORD. In Exodus 6, God assures them of victory and spells out His promises of deliverance. He says in 6:6-7 that He will: <u>bring them out</u> from their burdens; <u>deliver them</u> from bondage; <u>redeem them</u>; <u>take them</u> as His people. These four promises are symbolized each celebration of Passover. During the course of the evening's prayers, blessings and narratives that are included in the Seder[20], four cups of wine are drunk and each cup is associated with one of these promises.

In 7:3-4 God tells Moshe how hard his assignment will be. He never promises an easy road for His servants! Note that in verse 4 he says He will bring out His '*tzvaot*', which may be translated as 'hosts', but also means 'armies'. A bunch of scared slaves! But God sees what we can become!

Finally, in 7:20, the first plague, the first judgement on Egypt, is enacted. And it is the Nile, the source of life for the Egyptians and the source of death for the Hebrew male babies that received that first judgement.

---

[20] A word that means 'order' and is the name of the meal that begins Pesach, the Feast of the Passover.

The word translated plague is translated from '*negah*', which has the connotation of 'striking against'. Numbers 33:4 makes it clear that it was on the so-called gods of Egypt, that the God of Israel was executing judgement. *"...Also on their gods the LORD had executed judgments."*

## Exodus 8 & 9
## God in Control

In 8:1, the English translation is usually 'Go to Pharaoh...' but the Hebrew is actually 'Come to Pharaoh...'. Pharaoh thought he was in control but God was there in the Throne Room!

Following more plagues, the magicians realised that this power was way beyond them, belonging to a much higher Authority. However, Pharaoh's heart grew hard and he continued to harden his heart after each plague until the plague of boils in 9:10-12. Then the LORD hardened his heart as he said He would. It was a strengthening of what Pharaoh had already started himself. Like a habit that forms until it is almost impossible to break. A stark warning to mankind that continual hardening of the heart against God's Word will result in the LORD no longer speaking to that heart. *"I will not always strive with man,"* He said way back in Genesis 6:3. And Hebrews 3:8, which quotes Psalm 95:8, warns us not to harden our hearts. *"Do not harden your hearts as in the rebellion, In the day of trial in the wilderness."*

In Genesis 8:22, a separation was made. The plagues would no longer affect the land of Goshen where the Hebrews lived.

It is interesting to note that although in Exodus chapters 7 and 8 when magicians are mentioned, they are not named. Yet in 2 Timothy 3:8, they are, *"Now as Jannes and Jambres resisted Moses..."* This is another example of the writers of the New Testament quoting from the 'oral law[21]', now part of the Talmud[22].

## Exodus 10 & 11
## Judgement

The drama of the plagues continues throughout these chapters as disaster after disaster befalls Egypt.

In 11:4-5, Moshe passes on the terrible warning from the LORD that every firstborn will die, from the prince in the palace to the one that grinds the grain, meaning the lowliest servant.

## Exodus 12 & 13
## Elevated from Slavery to Freedom

An important principle is seen here. The people of God were the servants of God. They were not meant to be serving another power. Leviticus 25:42 says that if someone is so poor he sells

---

[21] A very short explanation is that the Oral Law is a legal commentary on the Torah, explaining how the commandments should be carried out. (Jewish Virtual Library)

[22] Talmud is the generic term for the documents that comment and expand upon the Mishnah, the first work of rabbinic law, published around the year 200 CE by Rabbi Judah the Patriarch in the land of Israel.

himself as a slave; a fellow Israelite was to redeem him. *"For they are My servants, whom I brought out of the land of Egypt; they shall not be sold as slaves after he is sold he may be redeemed again. One of his brothers may redeem him…"*

In Romans 6, Paul makes it clear that as servants of God, we are no longer slaves to another power – that of sin.

It was time for the chosen people of God to be delivered from a false master. Now we see something that God began in Genesis - the setting apart of His people for His redemptive purpose. It was done with great drama. And it is enacted each year as the Jewish nation celebrates Passover/*Pesach*, the beginning of redemption.

Chapters 12 and 13 of Exodus spell out many details concerning the observance of that first and future Passovers and is worth a study on its own. The deliverance from Egypt is referred to many times in Scripture and the commandment to remember what was done for them at this time is repeated in these chapters and other places. We will note only the instruction in 12:19, *"… no leaven shall be found in your houses."*

In 1 Corinthians 5:7, Believers are urged to clean out the old leaven, that is, that which puffs up, or which is corrupting. *"Therefore purge out the old leaven, that you may be a new lump, since you truly are unleavened. For indeed Messiah, our Passover, was sacrificed for us."* Paul bases this instruction on the Pesach preparations which includes cleaning the home thoroughly in order to be rid of any leaven – *hametz* in Hebrew – in accordance with God's instructions in Exodus 12:15, 19 and elsewhere. Those instructions are obeyed thoroughly by the observant Jewish household to ensure that there is no undetected crumb of *hametz* in some little corner. In the same way we need to apply Paul's instructions to the hidden corners of our lives.

That first Passover was only the beginning of true freedom. One of the names the Jewish people use to refer to Pesach is, The Time of Our Freedom, *Zeman Cherutenu*, because, 'God brought us *'me-avdut le-cherut'*, 'from slavery to freedom'. However, *'cherut'* is not the usual word for 'freedom'.

There are other Hebrew words for freedom, or liberty, depending on the context. They are:

- In Exodus 21:2 *chofesh*, is used in connection with the freeing of slaves.

- In Leviticus 25:10, *dror* is used in connection with the Jubilee year, *"...and proclaim liberty [dror] throughout all the land to all its inhabitants..."*

- However, the Sages coined a new word to describe the freedom that the Exodus brought. Here is the passage in which it occurs: *"The tablets were the work of God, and the writing was the writing of God, engraved [charut] on the tablets"* (Exodus. 32:16).

Unlike the English language, the lack of vowels in Hebrew allows for flexibility in the way that words can be pronounced. A slight change of pronunciation can change the meaning of the word depending on the context. This is what the sages did with the word for engraved. In Avot[23] 6:2 it says, 'Read not 'ch<u>a</u>rut', 'engraved' but ch<u>e</u>rut, 'freedom', for the only person who is truly free is one who occupies himself with Torah study'.

So how did a word that means 'engraved' come to mean 'freedom', and how is it related to the Torah in the eyes of the Jewish sages?

*Chofesh* is what a slave becomes when he or she goes free. It means that they can do what they like now. There is no one to order them around. However, freedom without constraint usually degenerates into lawlessness. We read in the last verse of the book of Judges: *"In those days there was no king in Israel; everyone did that which was right in his own eyes."*

Therefore, we can unite law (Torah) which they would soon receive, and liberty.

Consider two forms of writing in ancient times, the Sages say - one is to use ink on parchment (external), another is to engrave (*charut*) words in stone. It becomes part of the stone and cannot easily be obliterated.

The people of Israel were led out from Egypt into freedom, but unrestrained freedom can lead to lawlessness and its consequences. The Torah -the Divine Instructions of God - was given to curb a lack of restraint. The sages believed that the

---

[23] Pirkei Avot, which translates to English as Ethics of the Fathers, is a compilation of the ethical teachings and maxims of the Rabbis of the Mishnaic period which followed the destruction of the Temple in 70 AD

covenant that Jeremiah 31:31-33 was referring to, ("*...This is the covenant I will make with the house of Israel after that time - declares the Lord - I will put My law in their minds and write it on their hearts...*" Jeremiah 31:33), came into being when the Jews returned after the Babylonian exile. While this prophetic word has a much wider and deeper fulfilment to come, it is true that lessons were learned in the Exile and the people realised that their lack of heart commitment had led them into idolatry.

In spite of common Christian perceptions, the Jewish Rabbis have always understood that keeping God's commandments must be from the heart and not as a routine, legalistic manner. Psalm 119:11, "*Your word I have hidden in my heart, That I might not sin against You,*" and many other verses, particularly from that psalm, make it clear that Torah observance is a heart thing, it comes from a love of God and fellow man.

A truly free society is one where people keep the law because they care about the common good.

We must stand fast in the liberty or freedom we have been given. Galatians 5:1 tells us, "*Stand fast therefore in the liberty by which Messiah has made us free, and do not be entangled again with a yoke of bondage.*" That is, freedom from sin's control. Not freedom from obedience. As non-Jewish Believers in the God of Israel, we were never 'under the law/Torah' given through Moses to Israel with its many details that impacted on their daily lives. However, we are bound to follow the Divine principles and patterns embedded within the Torah, for a guide to holy living.

# Exodus 14 & 15
# Fear or Faith?

In 14:8 the Israelites went out with boldness, but that soon turned to panic as their way forward was blocked by the Sea of Reeds/*Yam Suph* (usually translated inaccurately as the Red Sea), and the way back by the Egyptian army. In fact, because they were following the pillar of cloud and pillar of fire, it was God who had them hemmed in. Perhaps He had made a terrible mistake, or perhaps, He wanted them to learn, He was in always in control.

In 14:15, they had to take the first step. So often in learning to trust God, we must take that first step of faith. Fear turned into victory as they praised God for His deliverance. It is good to note that in future accounts of this event, there is no more glorification of the drowning of the Egyptians. In Jewish writings there is a midrash[24] which tells of the angels rejoicing over the drowning army and God rebukes them asking how they can rejoice when His creatures are drowning. *"As surely as I live, declares the Sovereign LORD, I take no pleasure in the death of the wicked, but rather that they turn from their ways and live,"* states Ezekiel in 33:11.

In the song of 15:18, the Jewish Sages say, is the first reference to the Kingdom of God - *"the LORD shall reign forever and ever."* Someone 'reigning' denotes kingship and a kingdom. And it is an eternal Kingdom! In the Gospels Yeshua taught a lot about the Kingdom of Heaven/Kingdom of God. He showed how it

---

[24] A very simple explanation of Midrash is that it is commentary and can include stories to illustrate the meaning of a Biblical text.

was for the here and now, and how best to enter and remain part of it. One day it will be manifest on earth, *"Then I heard a loud voice saying in heaven, 'Now salvation, and strength, and the kingdom of our God, and the power of His Christ have come, for the accuser of our brethren, who accused them before our God day and night, has been cast down'."* Revelation 12:10

In 1 Corinthians 10:1-2, the experience of passing through the waters of Yam Suph, as well as being enveloped in the Cloud of the LORD, was likened by Paul to Baptism. *"Moreover, brethren, I do not want you to be unaware that all our fathers were under the cloud, all passed through the sea, all were baptized into Moses in the cloud and in the sea."*

But soon the trials began. In 15:22 to 26, there was only bitter water to drink. Have we tasted only bitter water in spite of following our Master? Perhaps this poem will explain why.

**MARAH** by Maxine Carlill

This water is too bitter; what can I drink instead?
I can't believe into this desert place, You've led
my steps, to where only bitter waters lie.
To a wilderness of loneliness, and hurt, and feeling dry.

I want to walk on soft and easy paths of green
that forever wind along beside a flowing stream
of sweet tasting water, then I won't complain
but drink my fill and refreshed, go on my way again.

My way, but perhaps not Yours. Your way is always right!
Perhaps you want for me, to be in this lonely site -
To thirst for You alone and accept whatever's from your hand -

Even bitter waters! One day I'll understand.

And so I kneel to drink and even as I bow,
the waters sweeter turn and I can only wonder how -
Until in the waters before me, I behold a Tree!
And know it represents the bitterness You've tasted already for me.

## Exodus 16 & 17
## Provision and Protection in a Desert Place

In chapter 16 the remarkable provision of the manna established a further lesson of trusting God's word. Rather than gather it according to instructions in 16:16-26, that is to gather it day by day and trust that it would remain fresh for the seventh day, some just had to test God, to see if He really meant what He said! The double portion of manna that fell each Friday is remembered in Jewish households each Friday night when the Sabbath/*Shabbat*, is welcomed. Two loaves of the plaited bread called *challa* are on the table and are covered by a cloth representing the dew which brought their daily supply of this heavenly bread in the wilderness.

In 17:1-7, more water problems soon emerge and, unbelievably again, lack of trust that God is able to provide is still evident. However, again God miraculously provides life-giving water from a seemingly lifeless rock, as Moshe strikes it in accordance with God's command.

In 1 Corinthians 10:4, Paul quotes a midrash[25] which says that a rock followed the people of Israel to provide water. Paul says, *"...For they drank of that spiritual Rock that followed them, and that Rock was Christ"*. Another example of how the New Testament drew on the Oral Law. Paul teaches that it represented Messiah who would one day be ever-present as The Rock. *"Jesus answered and said unto her, Whoever drinks of this water shall thirst again: But whoever drinks of the water that I shall give him shall never thirst; but the water that I shall give him shall be in him a well of water springing up into everlasting life."* John 4:13-14.

In Exodus 17:8-15, we read of the first test the Israelites had as free people to defend themselves. Even so, it required Moshe's silent intercession. As long as his hands were lifted to heaven in a gesture of petition, they prevailed. They were facing a cowardly and cunning enemy as Deuteronomy points out in 25:17 to18, *"Remember what Amalek did to you on the way as you were coming out of Egypt, how he met you on the way and attacked your rear ranks, all the stragglers at your rear, when you were tired and weary; and he did not fear God."* Beware of times of weariness!

It is also interesting to note that when it says in the latter part of Exodus 17:12, *"...and his [Moshe's] hands were steady..."* the word translated 'steady' is the Hebrew word *'emunah'*. It is the first time it appears in the Bible and is the word usually translated 'faith'. Therefore, it is a good reminder that faith involves remaining steadfast. The word 'amen' is the root of

---

[25] A simple explanation of Midrash is that it is commentary and can include stories to illustrate the meaning of a Biblical text.

*emunah* so when we say 'amen' to a prayer, we affirm our trust in a faithful God.

## Exodus 18
## Friends of Israel

It appears Jethro, in Hebrew *Yitro*, embraced the God of Israel after hearing of the miraculous events thus far. He offered sacrifices, and Aaron and the Elders of Israel ate a meal with him. His name, Yitro means 'abundance' and he was also known as Reuel (Exodus 2:18 and Numbers 10:29) which means Friend of God. His descendants, who were known as the Kenites, were afforded a special protection because of the kindness of Yitro. Let's not forget too that he gave shelter to Moshe when he fled Egypt. The Kenites were also praised by King Saul in 1 Samuel 15:6, "*Then Saul said to the Kenites, 'Go, depart, get down from among the Amalekites, lest I destroy you with them. For you showed kindness to all the children of Israel when they came up out of Egypt'.*" God also commended them through the mouth of Balaam in Numbers 24:21 for allying with Israel, "*Then he looked on the Kenites, and he took up his oracle and said: 'Firm is your dwelling place, And your nest is set in the rock'.*" A firm principle is established here. Taking a stand with the Jewish people is not unnoticed, especially when they face hostility. The nation of Israel, for example, honours each 'Righteous Gentile', that is, those who saved Jews during the Holocaust.

## Exodus 19 & 20
## Elevated to Nationhood

*"For ask now concerning the days that are past, which were before you, since the day that God created man on the earth, and ask from one end of heaven to the other whether any great thing like this has happened, or anything like it has been heard,"* Moshe asks in wonderment in Deuteronomy 4:32 as he reminded them of the dramatic and awe-inspiring events at Mt. Sinai.

No wonder that in Exodus19:10-13 and 19:21-22 there were solemn instructions about purifying themselves and keeping their boundaries. God spelt out His plans for them in19:3-6. He would make them His '<u>treasured possession</u>/*segula.'* (Sometimes translated as <u>special people</u> or <u>peculiar people</u>). Segula means an enclosed or guarded treasure, one that was the private property of the owner. He would also make them a 'kingdom of priests' and a 'holy nation'.

When 1 Peter 2:9 applies this same status to the new Gentile Believers in the God of Israel, *"But you* are *a chosen generation, a royal priesthood, a holy nation, His own special people (segula), that you may proclaim the praises of Him who called you out of darkness into His marvellous light..."* it is not a casual statement but one that needs to be treated with seriousness and a sense of awesome responsibility.

No other nation has entered into a covenant with God as did the freed slaves at the foot of the Mountain of God as described in Exodus 20. From slavery to nationhood! As a nation they received a Constitution! After receiving the Ten Commandments, or more accurately according to the Hebrew, the Ten <u>Words,</u> in 20:21, Moshe ascends the mountain and he receives additional commandments. These commandments are an interweaving of religious, civil and social justice instructions. This set of divine instructions was part of the covenant and are often referred to as 'the Mosaic Law'.

The event at Sinai is likened by the Rabbis to a Marriage Covenant. At Jewish weddings a written marriage agreement called a *ketuba*, is read out and the Mosaic Law was like a *ketuba*, they say.

In Leviticus 11:45 *"I am the Lord who brought you up out of Egypt to be your God; therefore, be holy, because I am holy,"* and, Leviticus 19:2, *"Be holy because I the LORD your God am holy."* God ensured that His Chosen People would reflect His holiness by giving them a lifestyle that was structured and regulated with boundaries and guidelines to help them live within His standards of behaviour.

Becoming a nation involved the following responsibilities:

* **Chosen-ness** - set apart, like the vessels in the temple. God required pure vessels as in Deuteronomy 7:6 NIV, *"For you are a people holy to the Lord your God. The Lord your God has chosen you out of all the peoples on the face of the earth to be his people..."*

* **A Channel of Redemption** – They were to reveal God's redemptive plan to the world. Within the Torah, the need

for atonement and the method of atonement was revealed, as was redemption through the sacrificial system, and its provision of grace for the repentant. Through the nation therefore, came the written word, and the Messiah, the living word.

- **A Calling** – a holy God demands holiness. Their call was to reflect a holy God to the world. To be a light to the nations as in Isaiah 49:6, *"...chosen you to be a light to the nations..."* It was the light of God to be later fully embodied through Messiah.

This Study will not go into details about all the laws in the following chapters, as instructive as that would be. We will note only a few points of interest, beginning with 20:25 concerning building an altar of stone. It could not be hewn with a tool, i.e. an iron tool. Iron is the material of weapons of war. It establishes a principle. Serving God should not be confused with waging war in His name, (although later we will study certain battles directed by Him). There are sadly, examples of this in Christian history, and today we see the same by another religion, causing suffering in many different parts of the world.

### Exodus 21 & 22
### Becoming an Ordered Society

Servanthood, a better translation than slavery, and of which we read in 21:1-4, was a welfare system for people caught in poverty. The system that God established within the society of Israel was just and humane. It bore no resemblance to slavery where one human being was owned and controlled by another. It was an opportunity to pay off debts or simply just to earn some money.

Exodus 21:5-6 seems to speak of loyalty and love. One can hear parallels drawn, and sermons preached, that this practice is a picture of becoming willing bondservants of our Master Yeshua. Interestingly however, this practice is looked at differently in Jewish teaching. The fact that a servant would forgo the opportunity for freedom and bind himself to a life of servitude is not looked on kindly within Judaism. Freedom is valued above all. As we know, the deliverance from Egypt painted a powerful picture of freedom and the cost of that freedom. The pierce mark in his ear marked him as a perpetual servant of someone and more of a mark of shame.

In 21:24 we come across the 'eye for an eye' statement and other physical wounds also seemingly demanding a harsh penalty. We will explain this further both in Leviticus and Deuteronomy, but know that eye for an eye was in the context of monetary compensation, as deliberate disfiguration of the body is forbidden by Jewish law.

The value of life, the value of other peoples' property and the seriousness of idolatry, are conveyed by Moshe so the new nation will be one of order and justice.

In 22:22-24, the injunction to care for the widows and fatherless would be a reflection on how diligently the community was obeying their Divine instructions. This particular commandment was a collective responsibility. Later, in times of backsliding, among the accusations that the prophets would thunder against Israel, oppressing the widow and fatherless was a primary one.

We will look at some of the commandments mentioned in these chapters 21 and 22 through to 23:19, in more detail in the later Books of Torah. Suffice to say for the moment, that they were given to a specific people for their unique calling. The principles that are laid down within those laws relate to religious obligations, relationships with family and the community, and ethical, civic and social responsibilities. Also, note that one only needs to read the New Testament, most of which was written to instruct new Gentile Believers, to see there are also many instructions, commandments and advice to ensure a holy lifestyle.

Ephesians chapter 5 has many such instructions for example, and says in verse 8, *"For you were once in darkness, but now, the light of the LORD. Walk as children of light."*

## Exodus 23
## Elevated to Intimate Connections to God

### Sacred Time

God gave His people a wonderful gift, their own calendar. As slaves, they had no control over time but in Exodus 12:2 when He was about to deliver them from slavery, He said that month would be the beginning of months for them.

Exodus 23:14 states that *"three times a year you shall keep a feast to Me."* Verse 17 orders all males to appear before the

LORD. Once within the Promised Land, they had to go up to the Temple in Jerusalem to celebrate these three Feasts.

The Passover, the first Feast, would be a day of memorial for them to keep year after year, to remember the deliverance from bondage. It is the day that Yeshua laid his life down to redeem all from the bondage of sin's grip.

In 23:16 the next Feast mentioned is called *hag hakatzir,* the Feast of Harvest. It was the first fruits of the harvest. In Leviticus 23:16, the timing was given – 50 days after Passover. In Numbers 28:26 it is called the 'Feast of Weeks', '*Shavuot*'. The Jewish sages say that the journey from deliverance to Mt Sinai took 50 days, so it is also a celebration of the giving of the Torah to the new nation. Because God works according to patterns, it is no coincidence that the outpouring of the Holy Spirit/*Ruach HaKodesh* on the Believers in Yeshua as the Messiah, (the first fruits of a spiritual harvest) was on the day of Pentecost/*Shavuot,* Acts 2:1-4.

Exodus 23:16 also speaks of the final harvest, here called the Feast of the Ingathering. Leviticus 23:34-43 calls it *Succot,* the Feast of Tabernacles, or Booths, and combines it with remembering their journey in the wilderness. It is a time of remembering God's provision and protection no matter how temporary their shelters were, and looks forward to a time when we will abide in His tabernacle forever, as Psalm 61:4 says, "*I will abide in Your tabernacle forever; I will trust in the shelter of Your wings.*"

These festivals and the weekly Shabbat, God made sacred 'time spans' and gave them to the Jewish people. They are known as *Moadim*, or, the LORD's appointed times, and are 'appointments with God' for His people to honour Him. (*"Give this command to the Israelites and say to them: Make sure you present to me at the appointed time/moad...*" Numbers 28:2, NIV). This meant they had to take control over time, to set these times apart, putting aside their business and whatever other claims time had on them.

The festivals are also known as *hagim* (plural for *hag*) which comes from the word for 'circle' because the year is a cycle, each 'appointment with God' re-enacting and remembering how God delivered them and established them as a nation.

It is interesting that God who is outside time, created time and put man within the framework of time. This means that we are limited by, and hedged in by, time. We are powerless against time. Yeshua said in Matthew 6:27 NIV, *"...who ...can add a single hour to his life?"*

Taking control over time was just one of the ways that His commandments kept them focused on the God they served. Living by the Torah taught them control over that which can distract from Godly living. Circumcision, for example, was symbolic of taking control over natural impulses and directing them within the framework of God's guidelines for holy living. The dietary laws referred to as *'kashrut'*, taught them to take control over the flesh. Keeping appointments with God taught them control over time.

## Exodus 24
## Intimate Fellowship with God

Exodus 24:1-2, 9-11, tells of an amazing event which Moshe, Aaron and his sons and seventy elders experienced. It is hard to imagine exactly what and how it transpired. Following the sealing of the covenant with blood, a covenant meal (24:3-8), which was part of the culture of the time, took place with Almighty God as the host. Another beautiful picture is here. That of fellowship! The LORD was not just a God of awesome power and miracles, but a God who desires intimate fellowship with His people, calling us always upward.

## Exodus 25-31
## Elevated to Partnership with God

### Sacred Space

Whilst on the mountain with God, Moshe received instructions for the people to construct a special structure, the Tabernacle. The Tabernacle in the Wilderness is called in Hebrew, a *mishkan*. It means a dwelling place or residence. Its details take up chapters and the significance of each one is a study in itself. The sheer amount of detail given means that surely we are to take notice of what God is revealing through the instructions, preparation, building, and functions of the mishkan. However, this Study will note only a few of the things of interest.

Up till now, the God of Israel has wrought miracles, signs and wonders on behalf of His people. Now He calls them into partnership with Him to construct something that will demonstrate more of the unfolding plan of redemption. They are to do the work; He will bless the project with His Presence.

The Torah speaks about Mount Sinai and the Tabernacle, both revelations of 'God's glory', in almost identical terms.

*"The glory of God settled on Mount Sinai. For six days the cloud covered the mountain, and on the seventh day God called to Moses from within the cloud."* 24:16.

*"Then the cloud covered the Tent of Meeting, and the glory of God filled the tabernacle."* 40:34.

The difference between them was that the sanctity of Mount Sinai was momentary, while that of the tabernacle was lasting. The revelation at Sinai was initiated by God. So overwhelming was it that the people said to Moses, *"Let God not speak to us any more, for if He does, we will die"* (20:19). By contrast, the tabernacle involved human labour. The Israelites made it; they prepared the structured space the Divine presence would eventually fill. Supernatural experiences are wonderful, but it is longer lasting when God asks us to partner with Him in bringing about His Presence in to the world.

In chapter 31:12-17, God emphasises His commandment regarding *Shabbat*, the Sabbath. The fact that it appears following the instructions about the mishkan and is delivered by Moshe just before its actual construction (35:1-3), makes it clear, say Jewish scholars, that keeping Shabbat is more important even, than building a dwelling place for God Himself. Therefore because of the timing of this injunction, the rabbis say that the kind of work that is forbidden on the Seventh Day encompasses the various activities that were involved in making the mishkan, the tabernacle, and these are the activities forbidden to the Jew on Shabbat. Modern life has stretched the list as new ways must be assessed to see if they profane this 'set-aside Day'.

An example of Sabbath observance is found in 35:1-3. The LORD, through Moshe, specifically banned kindling a fire which by implication stops all food preparation as well. Therefore, all meals for Shabbat are prepared by the observant Jew before Friday night, the start of this Day.

The responsibility to strictly observe Shabbat assigned to the Jewish people is because of the picture that God embedded in it. Hebrews 4:9-10, *"There remains therefore, a rest* (ie. a Sabbath rest) *for the people of God. For he who has entered that rest also ceased from his works as God did from His."* Although the life of those who belong to the family of God is an active and dynamic one, entering into that family is something for which we do not work, neither can we, because there is nothing we can do to make ourselves right before a Holy God. We saw in the Exodus from Egypt that the Hebrews were powerless to free themselves from slavery. God did everything through His servant Moshe. Once they were freed and set apart as a holy nation, there was plenty for them to do. Their new life was to be an ongoing partnership with God. So it is for spiritual deliverance, we rest in what God has provided through our Deliverer. There is nothing we can do to gain salvation but to accept and rest in the redemptive price paid for us on the cross. Then, there will be plenty of action!

## Exodus 32 & 33
## Descent into Idolatry

The appalling sight of the Golden Calf that greeted Moshe was another test for this great leader. God said in 32:10 that He would destroy the people and start again with Moshe. But Moshe was not tempted by that honour and he immediately interceded for God's mercy. He was truly their mediator (see 32:11-14, and 32:31-32), and was a wonderful example of compassion. This is what the New Testament urges in Jude 22-23 NLT, *"And you must show mercy to those whose faith is wavering. Rescue others by snatching them from the flames of judgment. Show mercy to still others, but do so with great caution, hating the sins that contaminate their lives."* Only God is the judge.

We may well wonder at Aaron being persuaded to do such a thing but in Exodus 32:1, the Hebrew indicates that when the people gathered around him, it was in a threatening manner.

Moshe's call for those to stand for the LORD, resulted in the tribe of Levi becoming the Priestly tribe with special functions they would perform on behalf of the nation, 32:25-28. Even though the ideal was for the whole nation to be a 'kingdom of priests' (Exodus 19:6), they forfeited that privilege in this incident of blatant idolatry, although in one sense they are a priestly nation in that they maintain a priestly role among the nations. Many Jewish traditions include rituals and prayers that reflect that calling.

So Moshe broke the tablets, written on by God Himself, and symbolic of the covenant the people had just broken. The tablets were not holy in themselves because only God is holy. They were the medium for God's Word and were broken because of sin. The people suffered judgement, 32:35, and in 33:3 when God seemingly withheld His Divine favour.

Then in chapter 33:4, at last, the implication of continuing without God's Presence finally dawned on the people, as it should whenever disobedience separates us from Him. The people mourned, and Moshe sought the LORD and begged for His Presence to with them.

"*Do not cast me away from Your Presence,*" David begs in Psalm 51:11 after his sin.

Note that Exodus 33:11, "*...the LORD spoke to Moses face to face...*" does not contradict 33:20 that says no one can see His face. The Hebrew word *panim,* is translated 'face', and in relation to God, also means His Presence. Moshe experienced His Presence as no other man had.

## Exodus 34
## A Forgiving God

In 34:5-7, Moshe has the awesome experience of the LORD passing before him and proclaiming His attributes. No wonder that in hearing such overwhelming words of compassion, in verse 8, Moshe prostrates himself in worship. He again begs forgiveness for the new nation and receives the assurance that the covenant will be maintained. More than that, he is told, the people of the God of Israel will be witness to a unique work done by the LORD Himself on their behalf. We should stop and read through the words Moshe heard and ponder on the God we have the privilege of serving. *"If God is for us, who can be against us?"* Paul asks in Romans 8:31.

## Exodus 35
## How to Serve Him

The construction of the mishkan begins with a call for all those with a willing heart to give, 35:5. Everyone had a chance to participate in this unique opportunity, to prepare a place for the presence of God. Having a 'willing heart' was the key. The phrase, 'willing heart' is repeated several times in the chapter. The Hebrew word translated 'willing' is *nadiv,* a word that means both 'willingly generous' and denoting 'a noble character'. Perhaps not all were so stirred and they missed this privilege, because in verse 22 we read that, *"they came both men and women, as many as had a willing heart."*

It's a beautiful picture of God's people, eager to prepare a dwelling place for Him in their lives.

There is a direction in 1 Peter 5:2 NIV to, *"Be shepherds of God's flock that is under your care, watching over them—not because you must, but because you are willing, as God wants you to be; not pursuing dishonest gain, but eager to serve…"*

*Maxine Carlill*

# Exodus 36-40
## Provision of Grace

The mishkan was constructed and from the outside it was not attractive with its plain coverings. However inside, the colours, the special items of furniture and the workmanship spoke of the beauty of worship. Compared to the account of creation, the instructions and then description of the building of the tabernacle take so much more space in our Bible. It is a picture of God's amazing grace! He wants to live among His people. This was a startling concept for the Children of Israel. The 'gods' of other cultures did not live with their people. They dwelt on mountains or in other remote places. But Israel's God would come down to their level.

Those who prepare Him a place according to His conditions of holiness can have the God of the Universe as a permanent presence in their lives.

I will point out two features.

One is that the outside covering of the tabernacle was skin, Exodus 26:14. The word is an obscure one and no one is really sure which animal it came from so badgers, dugongs, and seals are among the suggestions. An interesting note from Strongs Concordance explanation about the word, skin/*tachash*, is that ancient versions understood it to be the colour of (human) skin, although that is only conjecture. The idea though of skin covering the place where God would dwell combined with the timing for the construction of the mishkan – nine months – brings to mind the birth of Messiah!

Second, in 37:7-9, cherubim/*kruvim* which were winged beings, were sculptured and placed on the Mercy Seat of the Ark of the Covenant which represented the throne of God. Images of the kruvim were woven into the curtains that separated the Holy of Holies in which the Ark of the Covenant was placed. Kruvim were also placed at the entrance of the Garden of Eden when man was driven out. They were to ensure that man in his now sinful state could not come into the place where God's holiness resided. It was so in the mishkan. Their images warned that man could not approach the place where God dwelt. *"The LORD reigns; Let the peoples tremble! He dwells between the cherubim; Let the earth be moved!"* declares Psalm 99:1.

When the mishkan was finished, Exodus 9:32 says, *"Thus all the work of the tabernacle of the tent of meeting was finished. And the children of Israel did according to all that the LORD had commanded Moses; so they did."*

In 39:43, reminiscent of Genesis 1 when God saw His handiwork and declared it 'good', Moshe looked over all the work and saw it was done according to the LORD's detailed pattern. The people's obedience brought down the glory of God at the mishkan's dedication, 40:34.

We will learn more of the functions of the mishkan, the Tabernacle in the Wilderness, later in the Study, but for now, we just marvel at this provision of Grace. A law has been given, and its standards are high, but the Tabernacle was erected bringing God's Presence into their midst, and offered a way for each and every individual person to seek and receive forgiveness from God for failures and shortcomings. It is the place too, where the people, as a nation, will worship God and sacrifices will be brought for national repentance and in His grace, receive forgiveness.

*Open my eyes that I might behold wondrous things out of your Torah. Psalm 119:18*

# LESSONS FROM LEVITICUS

The pattern of separation and setting apart which God began at the beginning of the Torah, continues. The Hebrew name for this third book of Moses/*Moshe* is *v'yikra* – 'and He called'. This time the LORD[26] speaks to Moshe from the just completed tabernacle. The calling to Moshe and the people of Israel at Mt Sinai was to walk in holiness. Here, in this Book, we have further instructions laid down for God's set-apart people. Patterns of holy living emerge through the specific commandments spelt out for the Jewish nation. As non-Jewish Believers, we can take hold of the principles and pictures they form and apply them to our lives.

---

[26] The Four-Letter Name of God, *Yud-Heh-Vav-Heh*, is never pronounced by Jews because the correct way of pronunciation has been lost and they want to avoid saying it wrongly. It is perceived as a form of 'taking His Name in vain'. Therefore, in speech they substitute the word, HaShem, lit. 'the Name', and in prayer, *Adonai*. In English Bibles, 'LORD' in upper case substitutes *Yud-Heh-Vav-Heh*.

## Leviticus 1-7
## Provision of Pardon

There is one principle that applies to us as well as to the new nation. New life cannot begin without the provision of pardon for shortcomings and transgressions. These chapters begin to spell out the sacrifices and offerings that brought the repentant sinner close to God in order to receive a pardon. The many details given in these chapters tell us that they are worthy to be studied in detail. In this Study though, we will look only at a broad picture.

Hebrews 10:11 to 14 speaks of <u>one</u> sacrifice offered by Jesus/ *Yeshua*, and Hebrews 9:28 says, "*...so Christ was offered once to bear the sins of many...*"

In these chapters of Leviticus are five aspects of that one sacrifice:

Chapter one gives details of the **Burnt Offering** called in Hebrew the *Oleh*, meaning 'to rise up', because it was totally consumed on the altar and its aroma rose up to God. See Genesis 8:20-21, "*Then Noah built an altar to the LORD, and took of every clean animal and of every clean bird, and offered <u>burnt offerings</u> on the altar. And the LORD smelled a soothing aroma.*"

And Exodus 29:18, "*And you shall burn <u>the whole ram</u> on the altar. It is a burnt offering to the LORD; it is a sweet aroma, an offering made by fire to the LORD.*"

<u>A Burnt Offering represents total dedication.</u> Leviticus 1:9 speaks of a "*sweet smelling aroma.*" The Hebrew phrase *re'ach nicho'ach*, is translated in various ways but the full expression

is *"a pleasing fragrance to the LORD."* It is used over 40 times in the Torah. We can better describe it as a form of contentment for God when He sees the dedication, the commitment and the genuine heart expressed through the offering of the worshipper.

Ephesians 5:2 says, *"...as Christ has also loved us and given himself for us, an offering and a sacrifice to God for a sweet smelling aroma."*

Leviticus chapter two gives details of the **Grain Offering**. Like the sin and trespass offering, it was called 'most holy'. It was not to be offered with leaven which is a symbol of sin, especially the sin of pride, that which 'puffs up', or honey which can represent extravagance and luxury. Salt was added to prevent any corruption. It therefore represents an unblemished life. Hebrews 4:15 tells us we have a High Priest who is 'without sin'.

Chapter three describes the **Peace Offering** or **Thank Offering**. This was brought before the LORD as a confession offering, a free-will offering or a vow offering. It was voluntary and represented fellowship and communion with God. *"Being therefore justified by faith, we have shalom (peace) with God through our Lord Yeshua the Messiah,"* Romans 5:1 HNV.

The details concerning the **Sin Offering** are described in chapter four. Note that it was for unintentional, general sin. The Hebrew word for sin/*chatah)* means 'to miss the mark'. In other words, to fall short of God's mark, a condition of which we are very conscious. *"If we confess our sins, He is faithful and just to forgive us our sins and to cleanse us from all unrighteousness."* 1 John 1:9.

Leviticus chapter 5 through to chapter 6:7 speaks of the **Trespass Offering.** It covered the sins of defilement, 5:2-3, and the sin of careless speech, 5:4. The Book of James has much to say about speech and James 1:26 is especially clear on the sinfulness of an unrestrained tongue.

The Trespass Offering also covered sins against the LORD and His holiness - again, unintentional sin (5:14-19). But even if in ignorance, it was still sin and required atonement.

In 6:1-7 it was for sinning by falsehood, therefore involved other people. This offering had to be accompanied by restitution.

So, the Trespass Offering was for unintentional, specific sin, usually accompanied by restitution of some kind.

Note that there is no provision for deliberate sin. Hebrews 10:26 says, *"For if we sin wilfully after we have received the knowledge of the truth, there no longer remains a sacrifice for sins."*

Before leaving this brief outline of the provision of the opportunity for the sinner to restore fellowship with God, we should note two things. Bringing a sacrifice was a very public thing to do. One could not hide the fact that there was something to get right between oneself and God. James 5:16 says, *"Confess your trespasses to one another..."*

Secondly, even the poorest person could afford a means of atonement. In Leviticus 5:11, a measure of flour was enough; in this case, it was not a blood sacrifice.

Something important to remember is that throughout the Hebrew Scriptures, it was made clear that it was <u>repentance</u> that brought forgiveness. For example, Psalm 51:17, "*The sacrifices of God* are *a broken spirit, A broken and a contrite heart. These, O God, You will not despise.*" Also there are passages from the Prophets who warned against sacrifice and religious ritual without a repentant heart, followed by deeds that prove repentance, for example Isaiah 1:11-17, "*To what purpose* is *the multitude of your sacrifices unto me? says the LORD...Even though you make many prayers, I will not hear. Your hands are full of blood. Wash yourselves, make yourselves clean; Put away the evil of your doings from before My eyes. Cease to do evil, Learn to do good; Seek justice, Rebuke the oppressor; Defend the fatherless, Plead for the widow.*"

This path to receiving forgiveness is endorsed by the Jewish sages and rabbis. The sacrifices and offerings provided atonement/ *kapara*. *Kapara* protected the sinner from the wrath of God against his sin. They were to be accompanied by repentance and a contrite heart. The Hebrew word for sacrifice is *corban* which means 'to draw close'. The sacrifices enabled people to draw near to God, protected from His wrath, then, true repentance brought forgiveness.

Note too, that the sacrifices involved detailed rituals, expense of the offering, and a public declaration of wrongdoing of some form. In contrast, how lightly do we take for granted the forgiveness available through Yeshua's sacrifice? His effort, cost and public humiliation, should never be forgotten in our casual confessions of sin.

Thus, the first seven chapters of Leviticus deal with the sacrifices and offerings without which there can be no holiness. Because of this provision of means to restore fellowship with God following sin and shortcomings, God's people were ready to represent a holy God by living according to His instructions.

It is interesting to note that the *Haftorah*[27] of the 'Torah Portion' *Tzav*, Leviticus 6:8-8:36, is Jeremiah 7:21-8:3. In this passage, God through His prophet Jeremiah, reminds His people that walking in the ways He commanded them was most important because God did not give instructions about the sacrifices so they could continue sinning and have their sin covered; the purpose was to have an obedient people. Especially note Jeremiah 7:4, *"Do not trust in these lying words, saying, 'The temple of the LORD, the temple of the LORD, the temple of the LORD are these."*

Romans 6:1 says the same thing, *"What shall we say then? Shall we continue in sin that grace may abound?"*

## Leviticus 8
## A Holy Priesthood

### The Holiness of Worship and Service

1 Peter 2:1-5 HNV, *"Putting away therefore all wickedness, all deceit, hypocrisies, envies, and all evil speaking, as newborn*

---

[27] The *haftorah* is a passage from the Bible, usually from one of the prophets, which relates in some way to the weekly Torah portion. The first five books are divided into passages

*babes, long for the pure milk of the Word, that you may grow thereby, if indeed you have tasted that the Lord is gracious: coming to him, a living stone, rejected indeed by men, but chosen by God, precious. You also, as living stones, are built up as a spiritual house, to be a holy priesthood, to offer up spiritual sacrifices, acceptable to God through Yeshua the Messiah."*

In order to fulfil our calling as a holy priesthood, we need to know what a holy priesthood is! We can learn from the one which God established. Aaron represents our *"...great High Priest who has passed through the heavens, Jesus the Son of God...,"* Hebrews 4:14. Therefore, this role is not for us, so we will focus on Aaron's sons as our 'visual aid', to help us understand <u>our</u> role as priests.

- Firstly, in verses 1-3 of Leviticus chapter 8 the dedication of the priests was done in the sight of the congregation. It was a public declaration of who they were.

- Before being set aside for service, cleansing must take place. Verse 6 describes the washing of the priests.

- In verse 13 the priests were clothed with tunics, sashes and hats. The Talmud[28] (Zevochim 19) states: 'that nothing was permitted between the prescribed garments and the flesh, not even a bandage. He and his garments were one vessel performing the Divine will'.

---

[28] Talmud is the generic term for the documents that comment and expand upon the Mishnah, the first work of rabbinic law, published around the year 200 CE by Rabbi Judah the Patriarch in the land of Israel.

They were dressed by Moshe, God's representative, according to God's instructions in Exodus 28:41. Our covering must be the same. God must be our fashion designer. See Ezekiel 16:10 where God is so beautifully speaking of what He did for Israel, "*I clothed you in embroidered cloth and gave you sandals of badger skin; I clothed you with fine linen and covered you with silk.*" He set the pattern in *Gan Eden* (the Garden of Eden) when He chose the covering for Adam and Eve following their fall. In the *Tanakh*[29], the lack of clothing – nakedness - is a picture of shame, of vulnerability. Garments said who the person was. Examples: Psalm 132:16, "*I will also clothe her priests with salvation: and her saints shall shout aloud for joy.*"

And Job 29:14, "*I put on righteousness, and it clothed me; My justice was like a robe and a turban.*"

The New Testament continues with the analogy of clothing to teach spiritual truths, right through to Revelation, "*He who overcomes shall be clothed in white garments...*" Revelation 3:5.

• In Leviticus 8:14, the sin offering was made for their unintentional sin, see Leviticus 4.

• Then in verse 18 came the burnt or *Oleh* offering which signified their total dedication to God.

---

[29] TANAKH is the name for the Hebrew Bible. (Old Testament). It is actually an acronym formed from the first Hebrew letters that designate the divisions of the Bible - Torah, Prophets, and Writings.

- In verse 22, the second ram was offered and called the ram of <u>consecration</u>. The Hebrew word is *millu*. This word means: 'to be filled, be full, be accomplished, be armed, be satisfied'. It is related to serving, and in modern Hebrew, a derivative of the word, *milluim*, means military service. The blood of that ram was put on their right ears, right thumbs and right big toes. It consecrated their hearing, their actions and their 'walking'. But was not put on their mouths! They were to hear from God and obey Him in their actions; they were not called to be God's mouthpiece. The prophets spoke, not the priest, except to bless. James 1:19 says, "...*be swift to hear, slow to speak...*"

- Finally, in Leviticus 8:30 they were anointed with oil which represents the *Ruach haKodesh*, the Holy Spirit, and thereby were 'set apart' or 'anointed', for God's service in the same way the tabernacle and its vessels were set apart in 8:10.

- Then, in verse 33 they remained in the tabernacle/*mishkan*, in the Presence of God, for seven days. "*For seven days, He shall consecrate you.*" What a wonderful way to complete their consecration to service.

Titus 3:4-6 HNV says, "*But when the kindness of God our Saviour and his love toward mankind appeared, ... according to his mercy, he saved us, through the <u>washing</u> of regeneration and <u>renewing by the Ruach HaKodesh, which he poured out</u> on us richly, through Yeshua the Messiah our Saviour.*"

# Leviticus 9
## Exercising Priestly Duties

*Beginning Right*

Before they began their service as priests, there were some past sins which had to be dealt with. Therefore, we see further offerings in 9:1-21. Jewish commentators focus on two. One, the young bull or calf related specifically to Aaron, 9:2, and the kid of a goat for the people of Israel, 9:3.

The calf was a reminder and an atonement for the sin of the Golden Calf. The sin of idolatry that was committed in the wilderness! The kid of a goat was a reminder and an atonement for the deception of Jacob/*Yaakov*. He had worn a goat's skin to deceive his father. The priests represented a priestly nation and these offerings dealt with past sin in the nation's background. What is in our past that needs to be dealt with as we seek to serve in a holy priesthood – any idolatry, deception?

Then, as the priests stood in the gap for God's people and did all according to God's instructions, His glory appeared, verse 23. The people shouted/*ranan* - a ringing cry of joy and exaltation, verse 24. Obeying God's ways of doing things brings His acceptance of our commitment and service, and that always results in joy.

## Leviticus 10
## Exercising Priestly Duties

### Continuing Right

Nadab and Abihu, two of Aaron's sons, had been on the mountain in God's presence – Exodus 24:1, *"Now He said to Moses, 'Come up to the LORD, you and Aaron, Nadab and Abihu, and seventy of the elders of Israel, and worship from afar'."*

However, spiritual and supernatural experiences are not guarantees of maintaining an obedient walk. In the Book of Exodus within the instructions given for the building of the Tabernacle in the wilderness, the mishkan, were details about making and offering incense. It was offered on an altar of gold in the Holy Place. The incense was a sweet-smelling aroma, its offering symbolising worship and prayer rising to God. *"Let my prayer be set before You as incense, The lifting up of my hands as the evening sacrifice,"* says Psalm 141:2. In Revelation 5:8 and 8:3-4, incense represents the prayers of God's people. And indeed, in Numbers 16:46-47, incense was the intercessory medium to save the people from God's judgement for the sin of Korah's rebellion.

Therefore, when Nadab and Abihu took fire for the incense which represents worship and intercession, from a place other than from the altar of sacrifice, they spoiled the picture God intended. The coals had to come from the Bronze Altar of sacrifice to light the incense. The Bronze Altar was where sin was covered and the sinner forgiven. The picture that God has embedded in the ritual of the Incense Offering is that worship can be offered only after a right relationship with God has been established. Offering worship to God by means He has <u>not</u> ordained, results in His rejection of our service to Him. We must first come to 'the altar' where a sacrifice on our behalf has been offered to cover our sins.

Note in verse 3 it says that Aaron, the high priest and their father, was <u>silent</u>. The Hebrew word is *vayidom*. It is the silence of mourning the dead, see Ezekiel 24:17, "<u>*Sigh in silence, make no mourning for the dead.*</u>" And also the silence in the face of tragedy, see Lamentations 2:10, "*The elders of the daughter of Zion sit on the ground and <u>keep silence.</u>*" Some pain cannot be explained or understood fully, but accepting the sovereignty of God, as Aaron did at this moment, 'sanctified His Name'. (Note that the Jewish concept 'sanctifying the Name of God', something that should be done in all circumstances, was endorsed by the words our Master Yeshua taught us, "*Hallowed/sanctified be Your Name.*" Matthew 6:9).

Because the LORD in Leviticus 10:8 -10 warns against intoxicating drink when discharging priestly duties, some commentators believe that Nadab and Abihu had been indulging! An especially important function of priests was to maintain the ability to discern between holy and unholy, between clean and unclean. In Ezekiel 22:26, one of God's condemnations of the state of the priesthood at that sad period of a backslidden nation, was that the priests were failing in that essential role, "*Her priests have violated My law and profaned My holy things; they have not distinguished between the holy and unholy, nor have they made known the difference between the unclean and the clean...*"

When the writer of Hebrews rebukes the Believers for not moving on from basic principles, he says in 5:14 NIV, "*But solid food is for the mature, who by constant use have trained themselves to <u>distinguish good from evil.</u>*" Discernment, it seems, is maintained by its constant use. 1 Timothy 4:1 warns against listening to 'deceiving spirits'. How important then, to keep our spiritual senses in tune with God's Spirit.

We will return to consecutive chapters after continuing with the principles of a Holy Priesthood.

## Leviticus 21 & 22
## Holiness of Heritage

In these two chapters, there are specific instructions to the priests to ensure they discharge their duties in a suitable manner. The conclusion is that shame must not be brought on the name of the LORD, 21:6, 22:2, and 22:32. Nor must they bring shame to the field of service in which the holy priesthood is engaged.

Chapter 21 deals with the holiness of heritage because the privilege of belonging to the priestly class brought certain obligations and restrictions. The priests are to be free of defilement and again note that the association of death is an example of defilement because physical death is a picture of spiritual death. High standards with marriage and family are also required. There are rules from verse 16 onwards concerning the suitability for exercising one's priestly duties. Physical blemishes and weaknesses parallel spiritual deficiencies which limit the role that a priestly status demands. Hebrews 12:1 tells us to "...*lay aside every weight and the sin which so easily ensnares us...*"

Chapter 22:1-16 goes on to warn the priests to be scrupulous in maintaining a state of being clean before the LORD.

1 Peter chapter 2 informs new Believers of their priestly status, and continues with a list of standards of conduct.

## Leviticus 24
## The Holiness of Priestly Duties

Chapter 24 returns to priestly duties, one of which was ensuring that the light from the lampstand/menorah constantly shone from the Sanctuary of the LORD. In Matthew 5:14-16, Yeshua says, referencing Leviticus 24:2-4, "*You are the light of the world. A city that is set on a hill cannot be hidden. Nor do they light a lamp and put it under a basket, but on a lampstand, and it gives light to all who are in the house. Let your light shine before all men, that they may see your good works and glorify your Father in heaven.*"

How were his followers to put their light 'on a lampstand'? By good works! This is how the Father would be glorified.

The other duty, Leviticus 24:5-9, was to set out twelve loaves of bread in two rows in the holy place, before the Holy of Holies, the place of His Presence. In Exodus 25:30, 35:13, and 39:36, they are called 'showbread', or the 'Bread of His Presence'.

They represented the people's gratitude to God for His material blessings. Frankincense was put beside each of the two rows, symbolising prayer. This weekly renewal of setting out these symbolic items expressed continual thankfulness and the need for ongoing prayer for God to supply all their needs.

## Leviticus 11
## A Holy Nation

### Living by the Flesh or Living by the Spirit?

We will return to the earlier chapters now to look at an important principle.

Romans 8:5-9 NIV, *"Those who live according to the flesh have their minds set on what the flesh desires; but those who live in accordance with the spirit have their minds set on what the spirit desires. The mind governed by the flesh is death, but the mind governed by the spirit is life and peace."*

There is always a struggle between the physical, that is the flesh, and the spirit. In Leviticus 11 instructions continue through Moshe to a 'set aside people'. The dietary laws were the first set of laws following the formation of a priesthood. These laws represent the regulation (but not condemnation) of physical desires. Eating brought sin into the world and in this chapter, eating is the first fleshly desire that is dealt with. The first temptation of Yeshua in the wilderness was to break his fast. Eating can involve sight, (compare Eve who 'saw the fruit was good' before she tasted it). We can covet that which we don't need or is even harmful, in all aspects of life! We can indulge our appetite, rather than just satisfy our body's needs.

Note that eating and drinking are given as a channel for fellowship; it is an elevated function of human life. Think of that amazing covenant meal in Exodus 24:11 where the elders of the Israelites ate with God on Mt. Sinai. So, the dietary laws were not to give a negative aspect to something that should be enjoyed, instead, when eating is undertaken within the parameters of God's boundaries, it becomes a holy act, rather than an unrestrained indulgence.

Among the forbidden animals are those that feed on carcasses. A physical reminder that participating in things tainted with death and decay does not result in a healthy spiritual life. The psalmist prays in Psalm 119:37 *"Turn my eyes away from worthless things..."* And Philippians gives good advice in chapter 4 verse 8 to meditate on what is 'noble, just, pure, lovely and of good report'.

We must be aware of partial worthiness and not be deceived that it is 'ok' to be part of that which does not fully meet God's standards. That is why the pig is particularly representative of unclean animals. It does not chew its cud, but its feet are cloven so it has half the requirement for a clean animal. The pig's habit is to lie on its side with its feet displayed as if to say, 'see it is alright'.

Thus, the dietary laws are a good 'visual aid' of walking in the Spirit. We need to take heed of the picture that God has embedded in the separation of clean and unclean foods and we must be careful on what we allow our minds to feed. Colossians 3:2 advises, *"Set your minds on things above, not on things on the earth."*

Note that from verse 24 onwards, there are warnings of becoming unclean simply through contact with that which is unclean. These verses should alert us to an important principle – uncleanness is contagious. *"...keep oneself unspotted from the world,"* exhorts James 1:27.

## Leviticus 12 & 18
## Family Purity

1 Timothy 3:4 NIV, *"He must manage his own family well and see that his children obey him, and he must do so in a manner that is worthy of full respect."*

Ephesians 5:31, *"...a man shall leave his father and mother and be joined to his wife and the two shall become one flesh."*

Leviticus chapter 12 and chapter 18 are part of the purity laws that are spelt out in this Book. They specifically deal with the sanctity of family life.

The commandment about circumcision in verse 3 of chapter 12, which was already well known and practised, was a reminder that reproduction is to be within the restraints of God's purity laws. The seal of God on the male sex organ is a reminder that the people of God must refrain from giving in to natural impulses and animal-like desires and bring them within the constraints that God has instituted. Childbirth means family

95

continuation and the commandment regarding circumcision inserted in the middle of the commandments concerning childbirth is, according to Rabbi Riskin, the Chief Rabbi of Efrat in Judea, 'because the continuation of healthy family life is dependent on the sanctity being preserved'.

After childbirth, the restrictions on a woman required atonement; some rabbis say it is because in childbirth the woman touches death. The risks were much greater in earlier times. A female child means that death will be faced again requiring the double amount of time of a woman's separation. We will see that throughout these purity instructions, as well as other commandments, God emphasises 'life' and therefore anything connected to death, even something as wonderful as bringing life into the world was to be acknowledged and dealt with. Note that Yeshua's mother followed these instructions in Luke 2:22, *"Now when the days of her purification according to the law of Moses were completed, they brought him to Jerusalem to present him to the LORD."*

Chapter 18 continues with instructions that guard against sexual deviations to ensure that not only the family unit is protected, but also the community and even the nation. Wrong sexual relationships and deviations could bring not only defilement to oneself, but actually bring defilement to the Land of Israel, verses 22-28. And this would result in the 'judgement of exile'. The tragic picture of Israel in exile is a sombre one. It is better to avoid that which results in finding oneself outside the perfect will of God.

Chapter 20:10-21 also deals with sexual purity laws.

In Acts 15:18-20 when the Council of Jerusalem decided that the new Gentile Believers in Messiah did not have to formally convert to Judaism, four existing laws were passed on as a basis to begin learning holy living as well as to ensure fellowship with their Jewish brothers and sisters. Included in these four laws, was the commandment to restrain from sexual immorality, verse 20, *"...but we write to them to abstain from things polluted by idols, from sexual immorality, from things strangled, and from blood."*

It's interesting that as an introduction to Leviticus 18, God assures those who keep the commandments, that they will 'live by them'. His ways are always to bring life not death and sexual purity laws mean a healthy life for the family and therefore, the society.

It is also interesting to note that one of the readings during the Day of Atonement/*Yom Kippur* services is Leviticus 18. Some of these forbidden relationships were being practised in the world from which the people of Israel had been set apart, and on this most solemn day, this chapter is a reminder of the standards of purity and self-control that form Godly living.

## Leviticus 13 & 14
## An Outward Symbol of an Inner Spiritual Condition

Although leprosy is a common translation of the Hebrew *tzara'at*, it is not leprosy as we know and understand it today. Tzara'at is considered a visible mark of God's displeasure. In Jewish teaching, it is thought of as an outward symptom of an internal, spiritual disorder. It does not have a medical equivalent. Rabbi Samson Raphael Hirsch, (a highly respected German rabbi 1808-88) pointed out that because tzara'at was treated by priests rather than doctors, it shouldn't be interpreted as a medical problem at all, but rather as an exclusively spiritual ailment.

Nachmanides[30] viewed tzara'at as a withdrawal of Godliness. This explained why it could manifest itself in the walls of one's home. If someone sinned, and then began noticing green or red streaks on the walls of his house, this was an indication that as a result of his sin, God's Presence was withdrawing from his home.

The Talmud lists seven reasons why one might be afflicted with the condition: gossip, murder, perjury, forbidden sexual relationships, arrogance, theft, and envy. (Arakhin 16a). The Talmud though focuses on gossip, as do many contemporary Jewish commentators. They connect the word *metzora*, a person afflicted with tzara'at, to *motzi shem ra,* a person guilty of slander or libel. Read the story of Miriam in Numbers 12:1-10, and Deuteronomy 24:8. Based on this incident it is clear that *lashon hara,* 'careless speaking', is one of the sins that resulted in tzara'at. The sin of slander is dealt with clearly in James 3:1-10 which says in the first part of verse 6, *"And the tongue is a fire, a world of iniquity."*

---

[30] Nachmanides, also know as Rabbi Moses Ben Nachman Girunde and by his acronym, the Ramban was a leading medieval Jewish scholar born in Spain.

A saying from the Talmud agrees with his warning: 'Evil talk is like an arrow. A person who unsheathes a sword can regret his intention and return it to its sheath. But the arrow cannot be retrieved'.

The following are some principles we can learn from these chapters on tzara'at, as we think of spiritual conditions in our life or that of our community which may not be as it should:

1) Leviticus 14:3. The condition could be covered and hidden, but if exposed and confessed, it is the first step to redemption. In Psalm 51:3 David says, "*For I acknowledge my transgressions, and my sin is always before me.*" And James 5:16, "*Confess your sins to one another and pray for one another, that you may be healed.*"

2) Leviticus 13:4. Isolation was for the good of others so that the contagion of spiritual sickness would not spread.

3) In chapter 14 through the clear and detailed instructions of what the afflicted person had to do once free of the symptoms, a picture is painted of the repentant, like the cleansed 'leper', needing to show proof of a transformed life. In verse 53, letting a living bird loose outside the city and seeing that bird soar upwards, was a wonderful picture of the kind of freedom that freedom from sin brings.

Something to note in chapter 14 is that the *Parashat Hashavua*, (the weekly Torah Portion[31]), is called *Metzora*. Metzora is an Aramaic word meaning 'the afflicted'. In the Talmud[32] there is extensive discussion about tzara'at in which the Messiah is called by the Aramaic name, *tzura*/leper/afflicted one. In Isaiah 53:4, the Messiah is here identified with the 'stricken one', "... *Yet we esteemed Him stricken, Smitten by God, and afflicted.*"

## Leviticus 15
## Impurity Versus Purity

Bodily discharges, according to the Torah of Moses, brought a person into a state of impurity. Although these are physical and even natural functions and the rules concerning them obviously included health considerations, God is painting a

---

[31] The Five Books of Moses are divided into 54 weekly portions. The portion comprises usually a few chapters, and the full cycle is read over the course of one Jewish year.

[32] And the rabbis say: 'The Pale One of the House of Study (<u>Soncino translation</u>: the Leper Scholar) is his (Messiah's) name, as it is said: אכן חלינו הוא נשא ומכאבינו סבלם ואנחנו חשבנהו נגוע מכה אלהים ומענה -- "**Surely he has born our griefs and carried our sorrows: yet we did esteem him stricken (Soncino: a leper), smitten of G- d and afflicted**" (Isa. 53:4).' - <u>BT Sanhedrin 98b.</u> From the words חיורא (Aramaic) and נגוע (Hebrew), the Jewish translators rendered the Messiah's name in English as "the Leper Scholar." This is due to the association of נגע with leprosy (see the Hebrew of Lev.13 for example), and the use of חיוור by <u>Onkelos</u> to translate the Hebrew לבן that describes leprosy (Lev.13:21, 26, 42-43). This word association led to rabbinic agreement that Isaiah 53 was describing Messiah as a "leper". (From the web site: TAAM)

definite picture for us. A person can be pure or impure. An impurity can contaminate and cause the clean to be unclean. I believe the picture we see here is that which is outlined in *'A Guide to Understanding Biblical Hebrew'* by Rabbi Youlus, (see introduction). He points out that the word impurity or uncleanness is translated from *tumah* which means spiritual impurity or uncleanness:

'In Leviticus 15:31, the Torah summarizes the conditions of purity and impurity, "Thus shall ye separate the children of Israel from their uncleanness; that they die not in their uncleanness, when they defile My tabernacle that is among them." The key in this verse is the phrase, "when they defile My tabernacle." Because 'spiritual uncleanness' cannot coexist with the presence of holiness that is found inside the temple. Notice that every time the Torah speaks about the tabernacle, it says, "And I will dwell among you." The proper translation from the Hebrew is: "in you," and therefore it means that there is an internal sanctuary within our being. An analogy of this comes from a story of a common man who invites the King to his home to reside with him. This simple man invests great effort to embellish his house for the King. How much more effort should we invest when we invite the Almighty to reside within us? Therefore, the Torah teaches us there are certain 'impure' conditions that inhibit a person from being in the presence of Hashem'.

To continue, that which comes from <u>within</u> – wrong speech, wrong thoughts – can render us in a state of impurity. Sometimes we don't even realise it. We see ourselves as right before God, but impurity which can be hidden from others, can hinder our walk with Him, and bring contamination to those with whom we fellowship. Mark 7:20-21 NIV, *"He went on: what comes out of a person is what defiles them. For it is from within, out of a person's heart, that evil thoughts come..."*

Throughout chapter 15 are instructions about being clean of impurity, for example, 15:13-15. Being impure or unclean was not a sin, but not dealing with it, was a sin.

## Leviticus 16
### One Mediator between man and God

In the previous chapter, a picture emerged to teach us about the impurities of our hearts. Now we turn to another picture that God has painted, that of requiring a mediator.

In chapter 16 we see the high priest interceding for his people. It had become obvious that people required a mediator. Moses was their mediator. He would plead for the LORD's mercy at times of the nation's sinfulness. He was the one whom the people sent up the mountain to receive the law from God because of their fear. Now within the priesthood, in verses 1 and 2, God narrowed their accessibility to Him by stipulating that only the high priest, and only once a year, would come before His Presence in the Holy of Holies. This is a passage of which the detailed and dramatic rituals demand study to appreciate its full significance. However, in this Study, we will note only a few salient points.

The Day of Atonement/*Yom Kippur* was for the atonement and forgiveness of the nation, whereas the other sacrifices and offerings were for individuals or groups. Not only the people, but the sacred items of the tabernacle and later the temple, were also cleansed. Verse 16 makes it clear that uncleanness had penetrated even into the holy areas and it needed this annual cleansing to retain God's Presence, Who in His graciousness, dwelt between the cherubim in spite of the impurities.

The seriousness of the day was made clear in verse 29, "*...you are to afflict yourselves and do no work at all...*" Afflicting one's soul, the Jewish sages concluded, means self-denial which includes no eating, bathing, sexual activity or other self-indulgence. Although there is no longer a temple, Yom Kippur is still a solemn day in the Jewish calendar when the people follow the injunctions in verse 29. They attend the synagogues in large numbers for the long prayer services throughout the day, coming before their God as a community with confessions and repentance.

The high priest changed from his rich garments that denoted his status and role as the people's representative before God and went into the Holy of Holies on their behalf dressed in simple white linen. Yom Kippur worshippers today, often dress in a long white linen coat called a *kittel*.

As taught in the '*The Elegance of Exodus*', cherubim/*kruvim*, whose images were not only on the Mercy Seat that covered the Ark of the Covenant, but also woven into the curtains of the tabernacle and later the temple (Exodus 26:1 & 31), were the guardians of God's holiness. See Genesis 3:25 where they were placed at the entrance to *Gan Eden*, the Garden of Eden, to ensure that man in his now sinful state could not return. Therefore, the cherubim's images within this, another sanctuary, warned that coming into an earthly copy of the throne room of God in an unclean state was dangerous. Indeed, the nation waited anxiously for the high priest to come out safely, meaning that they were once again cleansed and accepted by a most holy God.

No wonder he entered in plain linen garments, a symbol of purity and humility. In Matthew 27:59, Yeshua's body was wrapped in linen, and although this was a burial tradition, it has extra significance when we realize that Yeshua was going to fulfil his role as the High Priest, and bear, not the blood of bulls and goats into the Heavenly Holy of Holies, but his own. Hebrews 9:12, "*Not with the blood of goats and calves, but with His own blood He entered the Most Holy Place once for all, having obtained eternal redemption.*"

That is of course, why Yeshua would not let Mary Magdalene/ *Miriam of Migdal*, touch him when she saw Him outside the tomb, John 20:17. He had not yet undertaken that High Priestly function ("*...I have not yet ascended to my Father...*") Afterwards, as we know, the disciples could touch him.

After the LORD, through the solemn ritual of Yom Kippur, made it clear that His people need a mediator, He provided one!

Hebrews 7:25-28 explains that Yeshua is our High Priest, saying in verse 25, "*... since He always lives to make intercession for them.*" And Hebrews 8:1 tells us that he sits at the right hand of the Throne of the Majestic God. We can approach the Throne of God seeking His mercy with confidence.

**UNDER THE GAZE OF THE CHERUBIM** (by Maxine Carlill)

Under the gaze of the cherubim
My God I come to You
And outstretched wings and flaming swords
Must part to let me through.
I bear the blood of Jesus
It is my only plea,
To come before a Holy God
And hear Him welcome me.

Mighty angels stand and stare
At this amazing sight,
A fallen human being
Now righteous in His sight.

The precious blood of Jesus
I claim it for my own
And boldly walk past cherubim
Up to the sapphire throne.

## Leviticus 17
## The Right Focus

Chapter 17 reinforces previous commandments. Verses 1 to 9 deal with the slaughter of animals for meat. It was obvious from verse 7 that sacrificing to demons was a problem. God had to change their corrupted mindset and direct worship towards the One God. Therefore, taking the animal to the precinct of the Tabernacle ensured there was no temptation to sacrifice to something other than the LORD. Once in the Promised Land these particular rules were adapted. Within this new walk with

God, idolatry was a constant trap for the people, as the Golden Calf episode demonstrated. How easy to do things our way and lose focus until we find ourselves 'worshipping another god'.

The Jewish apostles also had to wean the new Gentile Believers away from old practices such as in Ephesians 4:17-20 which included the entreaty, "*...to no longer walk as the rest of the Gentiles walk...*" Mindsets and established habits can be hard to change but, "*we have the mind of Christ...*" 1 Corinthians 2:16, and we must be open to new directions as the Spirit reveals ongoing understanding in what it means to be a set-apart people.

The rest of the chapter deals with the commandment that prohibited eating blood. The fact that blood is essential to life is indisputable, and its role in atonement renders it sacred.

I refer again to Acts 15 when the momentous and generous ruling was made following discussion about the Gentiles who were coming to believe in the God of Israel through faith in the Jewish Messiah. We can speculate that it would probably have been a heated one. The new Believers were from pagan backgrounds which included idolatry and debauched lifestyles. Should they be made to go through a *halachic*[33] conversion? That is, become Jews according to the ritual and standards that were demanded? Finally, it was decided that they would not expect that of the new Believers. However, it was imperative that basic principles of holy living were followed. It was also important to have guidelines for the Gentiles that would allow Jews to have fellowship with them. Therefore, basic commandments are spelt out in verse 20, and include the <u>forbidden consumption</u>

---

[33] The criteria of Jewish law.

of blood as well as idolatry and sexual immorality. As well as the letters from the apostles which eventually became the New Testament, there was an early document known as the *Didache*[34], (Greek for 'teaching'). It was like a basic instruction manual for Gentiles that prepared them for a new lifestyle. It reinforced the requirement to accept the rulings of the Jerusalem Council in Acts 15 and laid down other guidelines for living as a disciple of Yeshua.

It is interesting, that in Acts 15:21, it was acknowledged that Moses, (meaning the Mosaic law/Torah), is preached in every city each Shabbat. Implied in that I believe, was the understanding that the Gentiles had the opportunity to learn more of God's 'holy law', (Romans 7:12), by attending synagogue on Shabbat. Although the non-Jewish part of God's family is not bound by its legal obligations - its patterns, principles and pictures are embedded in historical narratives and detailed rituals for our instruction. The Torah is part of the 'all scripture' of 2 Timothy 3:16.

## Leviticus 19 & 20
## Collective Holiness, Individual Responsibility.

Ephesians 4:1, "*...walk worthy of the calling with which you have been called.*"

---

[34] This small book of 16 short chapters, was widely referred to by church leaders during the first 2 centuries. Since the manuscript was rediscovered in a monastery library in Instanbul in 1873, a growing number of Christian scholars and laymen are studying it's treasures.

Moses was to speak to the entire assembly of the children of Israel, Leviticus 19:1-2. The gathering represented <u>unity</u> and strength. However, everyone who stood there was <u>individually</u> <u>responsible</u> for carrying out the instructions to be holy. 1 Corinthians 12:27 HNV makes the collective and individual responsibilities clear, *"Now you are the body of Messiah, and members individually."*

These two chapters comprise the Torah Portion[35] named 'Kedoshim', meaning 'holiness'. The Portion occurs in the middle of Leviticus and is in the middle of the Torah. It is good to remind ourselves again, that God set apart a people to represent a holy God to a fallen world. Leviticus is sometimes called the Book of Holiness as it spells out so many of the standards to which His people are to aim. The very word *Torah* means teaching in the sense of giving direction towards a goal, and it comes from a root word *yored* which means 'to shoot', to 'find the mark'.

What follows now is a list of social, ethical and moral instructions. These include references to several of the Ten Commandments, further instructions about the right way of making offerings, consideration of the poor, justice and integrity and the avoidance of occult and pagan practices. This mixture of spiritual and ceremonial, ethical and moral instructions, Jewish commentary says, is because the Torah views human life as indivisible. The whole of life should come under God's sovereignty, not just parts of it. A careful reading of these two

---

[35] The *Parshat Hashavua*, or Torah Portion, is from the division of the Five Books of Moses for that week. The portion comprises usually a few chapters, and the whole Torah is studied in a year.

chapters will reveal <u>principles</u> that are intended for all those who want an idea of what living a holy life entails. Many of the specific commandments for the Jewish nation are endorsed in the many exhortations for righteous living within the Apostolic Writings (the New Testament). Hebrews 12:14 urges us to, *"Pursue peace with all people, <u>and holiness</u>, without which no one will see the Lord."*

It is by obedience to God's directives that His people, whether obliged to fulfil those directives literally or, as Gentile Believers, maintain the standards of behaviour they depict, remain truly holy/set aside/separated, for His service. *"And you shall be holy to Me, for I the LORD am holy and have separated you from the peoples so that you should be Mine."* Leviticus 20:26.

## Leviticus 23
## Appointments with the LORD

The feasts are elaborated several times in the Torah. They are visual aids, beautiful pictures of various aspects of redemption. Also, like the dietary laws which speak of control over the flesh, these appointments with God, these sacred spaces of time, speak of <u>control over time</u>.

This chapter, verses 1-3, begins with yet another reminder about the all-important weekly festival of Sabbath/*Shabbat*. This regular reminder is, as we saw in Genesis, linked to creation and the acknowledgement of God as Creator. It speaks of a Rest into which we are invited to enter. Hebrews 4:9-10, *"There remains therefore a rest for the people of God, For he who has entered His rest has himself also ceased from his works as God did from His."* We do not have to work for our salvation, but rest in what has been provided for us.

The observance of Passover/*Pesach*, verses 4-8, detailed in Exodus, was the beginning of redemption, release from slavery. In this passage, the commandment to eat only unleavened bread for seven days is repeated.

Immediately after Pesach, a sheaf of grain - barley - was presented before the LORD as a firstfruit offering. It was the first main crop of the year that was ready to harvest. Because, as said before, God works according to His patterns, the day that the sheaf was being waved in the Temple ritual, was the same day Yeshua rose from the dead. 1 Corinthians 15:20 *"But now is the Messiah risen from the dead, the firstfruits..."* By presenting a first fruit offering, it was like dedicating the whole harvest to God, acknowledging that it came from Him. Romans 11:16, *"For if the firstfruit is holy, the lump is also holy..."*

'Firstfruits' was an important principle that God instituted. As we have seen, the firstborn of His nation belongs to God, including livestock.

International Christian Embassy Jerusalem President, Jūrgen Būhler expands this principle in ICEJ's website www.icej,org, 4/25/2013 'Seasons of Harvest':

'God called Israel as a nation His firstborn. *"Thus says the LORD: "Israel is My son, My firstborn."* (Exodus 4:22). This means that Israel has been given by God the rank of the firstborn among the nations. In saying so, God declared in a beautiful way His intention to bless all the nations of the earth. Remember what Paul said: "If the firstfruit is holy then the lump is holy." (Romans 11:16)

In calling and blessing Israel as His firstborn, the Creator was declaring that He was also going to call and bless a redeemed people from all the nations. This corresponds to the election God placed upon Israel from the beginning: "In you all the families of the earth shall be blessed." (Genesis 12:3)

And indeed it was through the one "seed" of Abraham, Jesus the Messiah, that this blessing came to all humanity (Galatians 3:13-16).

But Israel's calling as the firstborn among the nations also gives hope for the restoration of Israel. Being the firstborn assured the privilege of a double blessing (Deuteronomy 21:15-17)'.

A countdown began after Pesach for 49 days, or 7 weeks, which is why the next festival is called *Shavuot*/the Feast of Weeks. It took place on the 50th day, which is why the Greek word 'Pentecost' (fiftieth), is used in the New Testament when referencing the festival such as Acts 2:1. Shavuot has other titles as well, one being the Festival of First Fruits/*Hag HaBikurim*, as at this time the wheat harvest is ready. It is the first ingathering of the harvest. Later in Deuteronomy 26:2, not only grain, but various fruits were added to offer before the LORD at this festival, and it became a joyous event. The Festival of First Fruits is emulated today by celebrations of agricultural produce throughout the country of Israel. It could not be observed by the new nation though, until they were in the Promised Land as only there could they grow and offer to God the fruits of His blessings.

Pesach was the <u>beginning</u> of redemption, symbolizing a release from bondage. Shavuot symbolizes an <u>entrance into a heritage</u>.

Shavuot is also called the Giving of the Torah/*Matan Torah* because the Jewish scholars have calculated that 50 days after the first Passover is when they would have stood at Mt Sinai. As God works according to patterns, it was this day that He poured out His Spirit on the new Believers (Acts chapter 2), thus establishing the New Covenant in which He would write His Torah on hearts.

Note what is inserted here among the instructions about the various feasts in Leviticus 23:22. In this verse is another reminder to share the bounty which God has shared with you, with the poor. The same principle was displayed in chapter 19:9.

Although hard work was required to produce a harvest, the harvest was still to be considered a gift from God. The Torah reminded the farmer of that here, and in other places, such as 25:1-9 when every seventh year, the land had to rest. To honour these laws, absolute trust has to be exercised to believe that God will provide enough through the fallow year.

Verses 24-25 of chapter 23 concerns the blowing of trumpets/*Yom HaTeruah*, which is, the rabbis say, like a wake-up call. The Day of Judgement follows as we see in 26-32. It is called the Day of Atonement/*Yom Kippur* which we discussed in chapter 16.

Soon after that solemn day, in 23:33-36, the joyous week of the Feast of Tabernacles/*Succot* arrives. Succot looks back to the way they had been protected and cared for when they lived in temporary dwellings during the wilderness journey. The flimsy shelters they must construct are an annual reminder that it is not possessions and circumstances that bring us security and contentment, but a trust in God to provide and protect. It is a foretaste of a day to come, that of eternally dwelling in God's Presence.

Pesach symbolises the beginning of redemption, a release from slavery; Shavuot is the realisation of all that redemption offers; and Succot - redemption completed!

## Leviticus 24
## When God Means What He Says

As we have already looked at the first part of chapter 24, we start with verse 10 which begins an account of a fight and a mixed race man blaspheming, or cursing, the Name of God. The judgement was the death penalty. Some biblical accounts are confronting and difficult to understand through the filter of our culture. However, God has placed some important pictures in the Torah in order for us to grasp concepts He wants us to understand with certainty. The same wrongdoing may be repeated in the future without such dramatic consequences, but the point has been firmly and forever made. In this case it has to do with His first commandment: not to take His Name in vain. The prayer that Yeshua taught makes the declaration that our Father's Name is to be hallowed. The hallowing or sanctification of God's Name is a strong teaching within Judaism. The desecration of the Name is a serious offence. It does not mean using the actual Name in a careless or blasphemous way only, but behaviour which brings it into shame, and at the same time, brings shame on the community of the people of God. In the passage at the end of the chapter, swift and severe judgement is brought on an offender. While the laws were still being established and conveyed by the LORD through Moshe, here was a situation where God demonstrated His standards once and for all.

Please note that the well-known phrase 'eye for an eye' in 24:20 and other similar phrases, was not a barbaric method of revenge. It is to do with justice. It was not followed literally, because for example – if I damaged your eye and mine was damaged in return, perhaps you are a surgeon or an artist or any profession that needs very good eyesight, whereas for me to have only one good eye may not be a problem, therefore, justice would not be really served. No, it has always been understood to demonstrate that suitable punishment and equitable restitution is part of real justice.

## Leviticus 25
## A Chance to Start Afresh

The Jubilee Year/*Yovel* is a continuation of the cycle of the set-apart time slots in the Biblical Calendar. The cycle of sevens is evident again as, after 49 years, the 50th is a Jubilee year. The land rested; it is a year of release from debt; a year of restoration and realignment. The Yovel was a unique social initiative that required a whole nation to cancel debts and restore property, and taught compassion and forgiveness. It gave those for whom life had taken difficult and unfortunate turns, a chance to begin again. With God, we are part of a community which emphasises compassion and forgiveness, allowing others as well as ourselves, to 'take heart with the day and begin again', as an old poem declares:

## NEW EVERY MORNING

Every day is a fresh beginning,
Listen my soul to the glad refrain.
And, in spite of old sorrows
And older sinning,
Troubles forecasted
And possible pain,
Take heart with the day and begin again.
*Susan Coolidge*

And Lamentations 3:22-23 KJV endorses it, "*It is of the LORD'S mercies that we are not consumed, because his compassions fail not. They are new every morning: great is thy faithfulness.*"

We must note that in Leviticus 25:25, we are introduced to the kinsman redeemer, *goel,* the nearest male relative to the person who found himself in a situation needing redemption. One of his roles, that of buying back land for a relative, is demonstrated in the lovely story of Ruth when Boaz bought the field back for Naomi. This is a deep subject, but we will not go further in this Study except to say that the earthly descendant of Ruth became our kinsman redeemer, redeeming us from slavery to the power of sin.

## Leviticus 26
## Consequences

The people of God have tremendous privileges and tremendous responsibilities. The blessings or punishments that are spelt out in chapter 26 are pictures of the consequences that follow obedience or disobedience. *"To whom much is given, much shall be required,"* said Yeshua, in Luke 12:48.

Leviticus 26:3 says, *"If you **walk** in my <u>statutes</u>, and **keep** my <u>commandments</u>, to do them..."* Physical walking involves the whole body and to walk before the LORD involves our whole being as the Torah has made clear through the range of commandments given to Israel.

'Statutes' is the English translation of *'chukim'* which are laws that are hard to understand. They do not have rational explanations but obeying them anyway, the rabbis say, is a demonstration of obedience of the Jewish people. It reminds us that <u>walking </u>in the path God lays down for us, however difficult, to understand is putting all our trust in Him.

Commandments, from the word *'mitzvot,'* are more understandable but can be open to ideas and influences. We too must <u>keep</u>, which also means <u>guard</u> in the Hebrew, the ways of God and not confuse them because of the twisted thinking of others - or ourselves.

There are other places in the Torah where the consequences of both obedience and disobedience are spelt out. Leviticus 26 is another reminder. But it is not a picture of a parent dispensing punishment and rewards, but a glimpse of the heart of God which yearns to see His people reaping the benefit of living in accordance with His ways. Psalm 81:11-13 confirms this, *"But My people would not heed My voice, And Israel would (have) none of Me. <u>So I gave them over to their own stubborn heart, to walk in their own counsels.</u> Oh, that My people would listen to Me, that Israel would walk in My ways!"*

Walking according to our own plans and 'wisdom' brings its own consequences, and often sad ones, which we see evident in societies who now scorn the words of God. Daniel, exiled in Babylon, recognised why he and his nation were in such a terrible situation. It is worth reading his earnest prayer of confession on the people's behalf in Daniel 9:4-19, which links their situation to the warnings in Torah including Leviticus 26:33.

*"Anyone who listens to my teaching and follows it is wise, like a person who builds a house on solid rock. Though the rain comes in torrents and the floodwaters rise and the winds beat against that house, it won't collapse because it is built on bedrock."* said Yeshua in Matthew 7:24-25 NLT.

As usual, grace is always there, and hope of restoration is always offered following dire warnings of disobedience. Leviticus 26:44-45 promises forgiveness and restoration for the nation of Israel. This is a prophecy we are privileged to witness literally in our day, with a greater fulfilment yet to come. Jeremiah 33:25-26 NIV confirms God's faithfulness, *"This is what the LORD says: 'If I have not made my covenant with day and night and established the laws of heaven and earth, then I will reject the descendants of Jacob and David my servant and will not choose one of his sons to rule over the descendants of Abraham, Isaac and Jacob. For I will restore their fortunes and have compassion on them."*

What a picture! And a guarantee of grace that is available for us following <u>our</u> failures. No wonder Paul could say so confidently in Romans 8:39 HNV that nothing can, *"...separate us from the love of God which is in Messiah Yeshua our Lord."*

## Leviticus 27
## Being Serious About God

This last chapter deals with the complicated rules of vows and possessions dedicated to God. What last picture can we see in this Book of 'visual aids' through this topic? I believe it is that God is not to be trifled with. A commitment to Him is serious and though abundant grace is extended to us when we fail, our heart intention should be a serious one. Luke 9:62, *"And Jesus said to him, 'no man, having put his hand to the plow, and looking back, is fit for the kingdom of God'."*

---

As you read through this most important handbook on holiness, do not become bogged down in the many rules and regulations which formed structures and boundaries for a nation called to be a light to other nations. Instead, glean from its rich pages, the principles, patterns and pictures that give the standard to which we are aiming.

Blessed is the man whom you discipline, O LORD, and whom you teach out of your Torah. Psalm 94:12

# WISDOM FROM THE WILDERNESS

The Hebrew name for the book of Numbers is *Bamidbar*, 'In the Wilderness'. The Psalms make several references to this wilderness period such as Psalm 78:52, "*But He made his own people to go forth like sheep, and guided them in the wilderness like a flock.*"

It is the Book that sees the new nation, redeemed, set apart, graced with the Presence of God, now setting out on a journey that will take them to the Promised Land and by doing so, enter into all the promises and fullness of life that God has for them. It is a journey in a wilderness, where the lack of comforts and even basic needs – food, water, shelter – will cast them on God's mercy. Their trust or lack of trust in that mercy makes up the content of the Book. The results that follow their decisions are clear to see. If we are wise, we will do well to emulate, or avoid, their actions so that even in a wilderness, we will know that we can count on God's Presence.

## Numbers 1-4
## The Counting of a Nation

Psalm 147:4 says, "*He counts the number of the stars, He calls them all by name.*" Our Creator cares for His creation, and He cares for individuals.

When God asks Moses/*Moshe* to count the people for various roles in Numbers, He uses the Hebrew term – *nasa rosh* – which means, 'lift up the head'. The person counted is honoured, he is not just lost in a crowd. Thus, each person had a place, and each tribe had its own unique role and place in the whole nation. There were also times that 'a census' displeased God such as in the fascinating 24th chapter of 2nd Samuel when King David ordered a census be taken. That is because God's people are not to be counted - or treated - as merely numbers to serve a purpose as they were in this case, but as individuals, each noted by God, with a unique role to play a part of a united whole. Judaism takes this Torah principle seriously. For example, when checking that there are at least 10 men present for corporate prayers which is the required minimum number, they recite Psalm 28:9 in which there are 10 Hebrew words, rather than count the men by numbers.

Rashi[36] says:

'Because they (the children of Israel) are dear to Him, G-d counts them often. He counted them when they were about to leave Egypt. He counted them after the Golden Calf to establish how many were left. And now that He was about to cause His presence to rest on them (with the inauguration of the sanctuary), He counted them again'. (Rashi on Bamidbar 1:1)[37]

No matter what their role, each tribe or clan was mentioned equally in chapters 1, 2, and 3 of Numbers, and again in chapter 7 when gifts were brought. What looks like endless repetition shows that one is not honoured above another. This is the example for the Body of Messiah. In 1 Corinthians chapter12, Paul very clearly spells out this principle. In verse 27 which we have seen before, he declares, *"Now you are the body of Christ, and members individually."*

Another clear principle is that order and structure and discipline are part of serving the LORD[37]. Being a part of His people is not made up of individualistic, random choices, of pleasing oneself, but part of an ordered whole.

---

[36] Rabbi Shlomo Yitzhaki, (Hebrew: רבי שלמה יצחקי), better known by the acronym Rashi (February 22, 1040 – July 13, 1105), was a rabbi from France, famed as the author of the first comprehensive commentaries on the Talmud, Torah, and Tanakh (Hebrew Bible). (*Online New World Encylopedia*).

[37] LORD denotes the four letter Name of God of which the pronunciation is unknown. Jews do not attempt to pronounce and refer to it as HaShem or in prayer, Adonai.

<u>Chapter 1</u> sees these ex-slaves being formed into an efficient army in order to face the opposition that would come against them. The minimum age was 20 years and included only those fit to be at war.

<u>Chapter 2</u> has to do with position. Each tribe had their place as directed by God. The placement was not of their own choosing or that of any man. Some positions seemed to indicate more honour than others. How easy it is to feel envious of another's position, to see someone receiving honour when we feel we don't receive enough. However, the pattern is clear in this and other passages - God does the choosing, the placement, the setting up and pulling down. The apostle Paul made it clear in chapter 12 of 1 Corinthians by using the analogy of a human body to explain that all parts are necessary and one part should not say to another, *"I have no need of you."* 1 Corinthians 12:21.

<u>Chapter 3</u> of Numbers, the Levites are counted and assigned their role. From the tribe of Levi, the priesthood was established. The rest of the Levites were to assist the priesthood (3:5-9). Just as Israel had been separated out from the nations, so too the Levites were separated out from the Israelite nation, in order to undertake a special role. The tribe of Levi had taken God's side against those who had sinned in the Golden Calf incident as related in Exodus 32. *"Then Moses stood in the entrance of the camp, and said 'whoever is on the LORD's side – come to me!' And all the sons of Levi gathered themselves together to him."* (verse 26). Therefore, they were separated, for the privilege of serving in the Temple.

Also, in Numbers 3:11-13, we see another role for the Levites. Israel was God's Firstborn, Exodus 4:22-23, *"Then you shall say to Pharaoh, 'Thus says the LORD: Israel is My son, <u>My firstborn</u>, so I say to you, let My son go that he may serve Me. But if you refuse to let him go, indeed I will kill your son, your firstborn'."* Indeed, Exodus 12:29 tells us this happened. Egypt's firstborn were the ransom for the slaves who were to be redeemed from captivity. Because the firstborn of Israel were spared from death during the Plague of the Firstborn, they belonged to God. God said to Moshe in Exodus 13:2, *"Consecrate to Me all the firstborn, whatever opens the womb among the children of Israel, both of man and beast; it is Mine."* In Numbers 3:11-13, and 3:41 and also in later places in the Torah, we read that the Levites are in place of the First Born who belonged to God.

And for those 'extra' Israelites, a 5 shekel redemption payment had to be made. The redemption payment was for each of 273 surplus firstborn Israelites over and above the Levite totals. Chapter 3:45–47 *"Take the Levites instead of all the firstborns among the children of Israel...You shall take five shekels per head, according to the holy shekel..."* Until today, when the firstborn male child of a Jewish family is about 30 days old, he is redeemed through a ceremony known as *Pidyon HaBen*. Five silver shekels, or equivalent in his country's currency, is paid to a priest, that is, a man whose family name identifies him as having been descended from Aaron. Note that in Luke 2:22-24 we read, *"Now when the days of her purification according to the law of Moses were completed, they brought Him [Jesus] to Jerusalem to present Him to the Lord (as it is written in the law of the LORD, '<u>Every male who opens the womb shall be</u>*

*called holy to the LORD'), and to offer a sacrifice according to what is said in the law of the LORD, 'A pair of turtledoves or two young pigeons'."*

The word *'pidyon'*, is derived from *'padah'*, one of the Hebrew words translated as redemption. Redemption, or buying back captives as spoken of in Leviticus 25:47-49, meant paying a ransom, it is part of the meaning of redemption. *"Now if a sojourner or stranger close to you becomes rich, and one of your brethren who dwells by him becomes poor, and sells himself to the stranger or sojourner close to you, or to a member of the stranger's family, after he is sold he may be redeemed again. One of his brothers may redeem him; or his uncle or his uncle's son may redeem him; or anyone who is near of kin to him in his family may redeem him; or if he is able he may redeem himself."*

Peter draws on the analogy when he says in 1 Peter 1:18-19, *"...knowing that you were not redeemed with corruptible things, like silver or gold, from your aimless conduct received by tradition from your fathers, but with the precious blood of Christ, as of a lamb without blemish and without spot."* We were also captives - but to the law of sin and death. (Romans 8:2).

<u>Chapter 4</u> of Numbers, the counting and assigning roles to the Levites continues. Within the tribe, each clan had their duties, again, some with more honour than others. We will look at one clan only in 4:1-20. The Kohathites had the task of preparing the items in the Holy Place and Holy of Holies for travelling. We could say they had the most dangerous job! Should they handle the items incorrectly, they would die, (chapter 4:20), hence the strict instructions concerning this duty. These physical objects

which were part of the ritual of the tabernacle, and later the temple, were holy/set apart because the tabernacle represented God's provision of grace, the place where sinful people could find forgiveness and where God's Presence dwelt. When God gave us such important 'pictures' through His people, His laws, His rituals and His objects, He severely judged those who 'spoiled' that picture by carelessness or any other way, hence, the stern warnings about handling temple objects carefully.

Pertaining to this reverence, Judaism treats scrolls or books containing God's words with great respect. A Jew will not place his Bible on the floor as Christians may do. Although it's the words themselves and not the 'container' in which they come that are holy, this outward reverence and respect is a lovely reminder of the holiness of the words inside, and an example we would do well to follow.

## Numbers 5
## Reminder of Holiness

Many of the divine instructions to His people had already been spelt out. The Book of Numbers deals mainly with their walk with God after finding their place within the nation.

Here in chapter 5 is a reminder not to forget that defilement, (and the bodily conditions in verse 2 are representative of defilement), is not to be tolerated within a set apart nation. Defilement, or impurity, was not sin. Not going through the ritual that restored a person to inclusion again into the community of God, was sinful. Impurities, even if by natural bodily functions, are connected to death of some kind and therefore a person is rendered defiled or unclean. (See *'Lessons from Leviticus'* ch.15). These contacts are sometimes unavoidable. Natural processes which required ritual cleansing perhaps involving inconvenience and delays to the day's plans, teaches us an important principle: that is, that uncleanness in our actions and our thoughts before the LORD must be dealt with promptly. Peter said in 1 Peter 3:15-16, *"But sanctify the Lord God in your hearts...having a good conscience..."*

Numbers 5:11-31 is the mysterious passage about the woman suspected by her husband of adultery. In the process of determining her innocence or guilt, the ritual involves obliterating the name of God, something strictly forbidden under other circumstances. The officiating priest recited a curse including God's name, wrote it on a parchment scroll, and then dissolved the writing in specially prepared water. The Jewish sages inferred from this that God was willing to renounce His own honour, allowing His name to be effaced in order to make peace between husband and wife by clearing an innocent woman from suspicion. Marriage is certainly a powerful picture of the relationship between God and His people, one used many times in the prophets and in the New Testament. Therefore, its sanctity was to be preserved. This ritual conveyed that message. It is interesting to note that this rather difficult to comprehend custom was brought to an end by the Rabbis two thousand years ago even before the destruction of the Temple. The reasons why are not completely clear but it is thought that the decision was due to social conditions at the time.

## Numbers 6
## Dedication

From the realm of marital suspicion and possible unfaithfulness and the attendant unhappiness that such situations bring, we move to the dedicated life. The Nazirite/*nazir* vow came from a desire to set aside varying lengths of time, the minimum period being thirty days, as times of austere restrictions in order to express his or her dedication to God (Numbers 6:2). "*...to separate himself to the LORD.*" The word *nazir* means separated. The vows could be for a variety of personal reasons such as thankfulness for recovery from illness or the birth of a child. Sampson was a Nazirite from birth, (Judges 13:7). It seems from Luke 1:15 that John the Baptist was also a Nazirite because of the injunction from the angel to his father in that verse about not drinking wine, something forbidden to the Nazirite.

In Acts 21:23-24 there was an occasion when, to confirm that he and other Jewish followers of Yeshua had not abandoned Torah, it was suggested to Paul that he pay the expenses of four men who had completed the time of their Nazirite vow and in keeping with the tradition to bring the payment to the priests. "*We have four men who have taken a vow. Take them and be purified with them, and pay their expenses so that they may shave* their *heads, and that all may know that those things of which they were informed concerning you are nothing, but that you yourself also walk orderly and keep the law.*"

Words vowed before God are not to be treated lightly and the Nazirite vow was a serious vow to be honoured by the one who undertook a time of serving the LORD and his community in this special way. In God's list of shortcomings of the northern kingdom of Israel, He rebukes them for turning away those who had a special calling on their lives, from that call, "*I raised up some of your sons as prophets, And some of your young men as Nazirites. Is it not so, O you children of Israel? Says the LORD, But you gave the Nazirites wine to drink, and commanded the prophets saying, 'Do not prophesy!'*" A warning to be heeded from Amos 2:11-12! Influencing someone to turn away from God's calling on their life is a serious matter.

## A Channel of Blessing

In Numbers 6:22-27 Aaron and his sons were instructed to give a blessing to the people known in English as 'The Priestly Blessing'. As in the days of the temple, the priestly blessing today is an important feature of the synagogue service. It is chanted in the time honoured tradition by men who are descendants of Aaron. Twice a year in Israel at Passover/*Pesach* and Feast of Tabernacles/*Succot*, thousands stand in the vicinity of the *Kotel*, the Western Wall, to hear the words spoken to the nation by those descendants, standing with outstretched arms under the covering of their *tallits*/prayer shawls. Although the words of the Priestly Blessing deserve analysis for their full depth of meaning, we will say here only that they speak of provision, protection, grace and love poured out, attentive care, and a peace which passes all understanding. It came from the heart of God to be given through His chosen channel, a holy priesthood. Not only is it a beautiful literal blessing that parents can pray over their children or churches on their congregations, but it also teaches us something else about the responsibility of a holy priesthood. The priests' responsibility was to ensure that people know the <u>intent</u> of that blessing even if they never hear the words. They will learn it only if it is conveyed through the actions and attitudes of a holy priesthood. It is similar to 2 Corinthians 2:15, *"For we are to God the fragrance of Christ among those who are being saved and among those who are perishing."*

## Numbers 7
### Unity

Chronologically this chapter seems as if it belongs after Exodus 40 when the Tabernacle was set up. However, it also fits with the picture we see in the various 'countings', the numbers, which gives the English name to this Book. Again, before God there is equality in importance. In this case we see the tribes who we now know had separate roles and positions and were different in size, participating in harmony, not outdoing the other, the whole nation united in purpose. By now God has given a very clear picture of maintaining unity and this is carried through to the New Testament such as in 1 Corinthians 3:1-8, where Paul warns the Body of Messiah against jealousy and claiming superiority. And Ephesians 4:3, *"...endeavouring to keep the unity of the spirit..."*

## Numbers 8
### Shining the Light

Even though instructions had been given to Aaron about lighting the menorah in the Book of Exodus 27:20, here are further instructions about that duty, rather curiously inserted in Numbers 8:1-4. It follows the list of generous gifts from all the tribes, except from the Levites and because of that, the Jewish sages suggest, the insertion was to assure Aaron that the gift of the priestly clan of Levites was to shed light. The angle of the light was important too, (verse 3). The light from the menorah was to shine at the entrance to the Holy Place, thus pointing the way into the presence of God. Does our life point to God in such a way? How do <u>we</u> reflect that light with which we've been entrusted - the way that God directs?

Also, in Numbers 8:4 there is a reference to the design of the menorah which was given in detail in Exodus 25:31-39 and followed up in Exodus 37:17-24 in which the bowls had to be made like almond blossoms. The menorah therefore, was to represent the blossoming almond tree, so we should pause and take note of the tree's symbolism.

The blossom of the almond tree is the first blossom appearing at the end of winter in Israel. Its pink and white blossoms dot the landscape pointing to spring, to new life. It is therefore, a symbol of hope. In Jeremiah 1:4-9, the prophet has been given a difficult assignment - to speak to his people with warnings and pleas to repent before judgement comes, even though God told him they would not listen. However, God assures him that in the midst of the bleakness of exile and suffering, His promises for Israel <u>will</u> come to pass. One of the signs he gives is the almond tree. It seems it is the season of blossoming at the time that He asks Jeremiah to look at one and Jeremiah replies in Jeremiah 1:11, "*I see the branch of an almond tree.*" God says in 1:12, "*You have seen well and I am <u>watching/guarding</u> over* *my word to perform it.*" The word translated 'watching' or 'guarding' is *shaked* the same letters, but pronounced slightly differently, for the word for almond/*sh'ked*. A play on words is common in the Hebrew Scriptures to make a point. Just as the sight of the blossoming almond tree promised the end of winter, so God's words assured Jeremiah that there was indeed hope for an end to the coming exile.

Later in this Study we will see that the almond tree on which the design of the menorah was based was also a symbol of authority and resurrection life.

**Ordained for Service**

In Numbers 8:5, to the end of chapter, the Levites are formally separated for service. They have already been assigned certain duties of which we read in chapters 3 and 4. Now they are publicly ordained. Sin is dealt with and they undergo a cleansing in order to be fit for the service to which they are called. In verse 19 of chapter 8, God gave the Levites back to the people. By serving Aaron and his sons, they ensured that the work in the tabernacle/*mishkan*, and later the temple, was done without endangering the lives of the other Israelites in that holy area where an inappropriate or a careless approach could mean divine punishment. Chapter 18:1-7 reiterates this principle.

Ensuring that 'unauthorised' persons are protected from the holiness of God is a regular picture that is drawn for us within the Torah. One example I have already pointed out is when Adam and Eve were expelled from the Garden of Eden/*Gan*

*Eden.* Cherubim with flaming swords guarded the entrance so sinful man could not go back into this 'Holy of Holies on earth'. This is why in the tabernacle/*mishkan*, images of cherubim were woven into the curtains and carved over the Mercy Seat in the Holy of Holies. These beings guarded God's holy presence in that place and there were strict rules about how the High Priest could approach it once a year. Approaching a holy God and that which pertains to Him was not a light manner.

Yeshua has opened the way for us, even as Gentiles, to come before a Holy God and call Him Father. Hebrews 12:18-24 tells us that we did not have to stand in fear before the dramatic and terrifying sight of God's descent to Mt Sinai, but we stand before another mountain, Mt Zion, which among other things speaks of worship. For example 2 Samuel 6:12-17 is the account of King David placing the ark of the covenant in a specially-prepared tent on Mt Zion and offering worship directly in front of it. Mt Zion is the place of Yeshua's rule, Revelation 14:1, *"Then I looked and behold a Lamb standing on Mt. Zion..."* Psalm 2:6, *"I have set My king on My holy hill of Zion."*

## Numbers 9
### Better Late than Never

The annual remembrance of Passover, their deliverance from bondage, was an important appointment that God had made with His people. However, the account of men who had become unclean before the Passover meal because of contact with death and were now asking for a second chance, tells us something of the grace of God. Verse 13 makes it clear that it was very serious not to avail oneself of this invitation and commandment of the LORD to remember His deliverance from Egypt through the celebration of Passover. Their sincere desire to obey God gave them the privilege of partaking in this celebration of salvation and deliverance even if they came late! Yes, as the directive in verse 10 demonstrates, there is a Grace that welcomes those tainted with death, those who are unclean, or those late because they had to travel from afar. *"But God, being rich in mercy, for his great love with which he loved us, even when we were dead through our trespasses, made us alive together with Messiah (by grace you have been saved),"* said the apostle Paul in Ephesians 2:4-5 HNV, wanting to explain a mystery that was hidden in the Hebrew Scriptures. The unfolding of this mystery had amazed him. How was God going to bring the Gentiles to Himself? It had been promised, but how would it happen? He discusses it in Ephesians 2:11-13. *"You Gentiles"*, he says, *"were once aliens, outsiders, far away."* Yes, we Gentiles were on a far journey. But we come, even if late, to being able to celebrate the deliverance wrought for us and that we, *"...are no longer strangers and foreigners, but fellow citizens..."* Ephesians 2:19.

## Numbers 10
## Moving on in Triumph

Final preparations were being made for the nation to move. Silver trumpets were specially made for the priests to blow indicating all was in order and that it was time to move out according to God's instructions. Note that although the *shofarim*/rams horns, could be blown for many different reasons, only the priests could sound the silver trumpets.

It was 48 days since the erection of the *mishkan* and the second year of their release from captivity. The stirring words declared by Moshe in verses 35-36 are recited in the synagogue at the point of the service when the Torah scroll is taken out of the 'ark', (the cupboard holding the Torah scrolls which is always located at the front of synagogues,) and held high for the congregation to see.

Those verses, *"...let your enemies be scattered..."* endorse a wonderful picture from this inspiring milestone in Numbers. When the people of God are on the move in accordance with God's will, our enemies will be dispersed.

## Numbers 11
## Warnings for Grumblers

Although everything started off well and in order, in a short time complainers emerged, and once again Egypt is mentioned with fondness and the supernaturally provided manna - angels' food as Psalm 78:25 calls it – was disdained. Note that in this case it was the mixed multitude that caused the unrest which obviously spread, (Numbers 11:4). In Exodus 12:38 we learned that a mixed multitude joined themselves to the Hebrew slaves, perhaps awed by the dramatic judgements on Egypt and the favour shown to the Hebrews. They may have included Egyptians as well as slaves of Egypt from other nations. There are cases where non-Israelites such as Jethro/*Yitro* (Moshe's father in law, a Midianite) for example, joined themselves to Israel in friendship, but for the tag-along mixed multitude from Egypt, it was not a heart connection it seems and Israel was in danger of being dragged down by them. Although reaching out to, and embracing those outside the family of God is our mandate, we are warned in the New Testament to withdraw from those who cause trouble among that family. See 2 Thessalonians 3:6, *"But we command you, brethren, in the name of our Lord Jesus Christ, that you withdraw from every brother who walks disorderly and not according to the tradition which he received from us,"* and 1 Timothy 6:3-5 warns, *"...he is proud, knowing nothing, but is obsessed with disputes and arguments over words, from which come envy, strife, reviling, evil suspicions, useless wranglings of men of corrupt minds and destitute of the truth, who suppose that godliness is a means of gain. From such withdraw yourself."*

Another warning inherent in this account in chapter 11 is not to look back! We should heed Philippians 3:13, *"...one thing I do, forgetting those things which are behind and reaching forward to those things which are ahead..."* The discontented saw the benefits of Egypt, if we can believe food really was in the abundance they claim. They looked back to a sense of security even though they had been slaves, controlled and owned by other forces. Now they were on an unknown journey, with a boring diet albeit a supernaturally supplied one! Rashi[38] suggests it was not the lack of meat! They did have flocks and it was possible that they could have eaten the occasional meal of meat. After all God had made rules for the Wilderness Journey concerning the killing of animals in Leviticus 17. 'No', Rashi says, 'it's about

---

[38] Rabbi Shlomo Yitzhaki, (Hebrew: רבי שלמה יצחקי), better known by the acronym Rashi (February 22, 1040 – July 13, 1105), was a rabbi from France, famed as the author of the first comprehensive commentaries on the Talmud, Torah, and Tanakh (Hebrew Bible). (*Online New World Encyclopedia*

being uncomfortable with God and the life He had brought them into. They would renounce their freedom for the old life with which they were familiar. They forgot the bondage'.

Life with God is not always comfortable. Yeshua actually promises persecution and talks about taking up a cross! Looking back to a more comfortable lifestyle is dangerous if being slaves to another master is forgotten. Chapter 6 of Romans explains to what we were slaves. For example, Romans 6:16: *"Do you not know that to whom you present yourselves slaves to obey, you are that one's slaves whom you obey, whether of sin leading to death, or of obedience leading to righteousness?"*

Moshe's despairing cry to God in Numbers 11:11-15, was heard and seventy elders were anointed to share the burden of leadership. This principle is an important one. Responsibility for this large congregation of people was not about one leader doing everything. Leadership is about shared responsibility, and the leader needs to be humble enough to accept help and also to share any praise with others. In Acts 6:2-4 the duties of pastoral care had grown too large to be done effectively, *"Then the twelve summoned the multitude of the disciples and said, 'It is not desirable that we should leave the word of God and serve tables. Therefore, brethren, seek out from among you seven men of good reputation, full of the Holy Spirit and wisdom, whom we may appoint over this business; but we will give ourselves continually to prayer and to the ministry of the word'."*

In Numbers 11:31-34 the LORD answered the complaining cries of the assembly about their desire for meat, but is not always a good idea to beseech God to indulge our every want.

The quails that landed brought meat, but also illness and death. These birds blown in from the sea as a poultry dinner for the taking, were probably among the huge annual migrations of birds across the Middle East. When quails are in migration, they will eat whatever is on hand, and one of the plants they often find is hemlock. Hemlock is poisonous to humans, but not to the quail, which gorge themselves. Eating quail at particular times results in terrible physical symptoms and often death.

## Numbers 12
## The Seriousness of Slander

In Leviticus 13, we saw the condition that is usually translated as leprosy, is in fact not the medical condition that we know. The Hebrew word *tzaar'at* is, the rabbis say, a spiritual condition which is associated with a number of sinful behaviours. The main one of these is *lashon hara* or evil speech. Contracting tzara'at was the judgement on Miriam for her disparagement of Moshe. It is interesting that the passage makes the point that Miriam was the colour of snow – the opposite colour of Moshe's black wife with whom Miriam and Aaron had an issue. Why was Miriam punished and not Aaron as well? The fact that she is mentioned first, say the Jewish scholars when the man's name usually comes first, shows that she was most likely the instigator. However, Aaron shared responsibility too. Interestingly, the fact that he looked to Moshe for mercy and help showed that he recognised Moshe's role as mediator.

The principle of avoiding slander as mentioned in the '*Lessons from Leviticus*' is endorsed in the 3rd chapter of James 3:9 NIV,

*"With the tongue we praise our Lord and Father, and with it we curse human beings, who have been made in God's likeness.."* We need to make sure that the 'words of our mouths and the meditation of our hearts', are acceptable to the LORD as Psalm 19:14 prays.

Miriam remained outside the community according to the seven day isolation periods spelt out in Leviticus 13 and 14.

## Numbers 13 & 14
## By Faith or by Sight?

A weekly Torah portion/*parashat hashavua*, begins at chapter 13 and ends at the end of chapter 15. The name of it is *Sh'lachah*, and literally means 'send out for yourself'.

It seems from Deuteronomy 1:22, *"And every one of you came near to me and said, 'Let us send men before us, and let them search out the land for us..."* that all the people asked Moshe to send spies into Canaan. It displayed a lack of trust in God's promise that He was taking them to a 'land of milk and honey'. They wanted to move by sight, not faith. God wanted them to trust Him but He allows them to do what they asked and therefore tells Moshe in Numbers 13:1-2, to send them (for yourself). Moshe sends them with specific instructions on what to report. The word *tur* sometimes translated 'to spy', is in other places translated as 'search out' or 'view', for example Numbers 10:33 *"...and the ark...went before them...to <u>search out</u> a resting place..."* and Joshua 2:1 to *"<u>view the land.</u>"* It was meant to be a gathering of information of their promised homeland, a fact-finding mission. But in spite of the miracles they had seen so far and their deliverances against all odds, courage failed at the negative report. Fear took over. Joshua 2:9 KJV shows that their fear was misplaced as even Rahab in Jericho had heard that the LORD was with them, *"And she said unto the men, <u>I know </u>that the LORD hath given you the land<u>, and that your terror is fallen upon us, and that all the inhabitants of the land faint because of you</u>."*

But it was too late! The report had a tragic and disastrous effect. A whole generation forfeited the will of God for their lives, and the chance to enjoy the abundance that lay waiting for them. We see here an obvious fact, well confirmed by modern experts, that negative words are harmful and soul destroying, affecting those around us.

I would like to point out another fact: that a bad report about Israel is a serious thing in God's eyes. Modern Israel and its people have many weaknesses and flaws, some of which must truly grieve the LORD. However, as Believers in the God of Israel, we owe much gratitude to the Jews who have paid dearly for being the chosen nation and the channel of redemption through whom God gave His Word and His Messiah. Therefore we need to be very careful in what we say in the public arena. We must see past headlines and the world's criticism to see the way God views His country and His people. Throughout the Hebrew Scriptures, God thunders His judgement and rebukes upon Israel, He alone is their Judge. But those dire pronouncements from God are interspersed with His promises of love which will never falter. He also threatens the nations who go against His beloved nation with terrible consequences. We do not want to find ourselves on the wrong side.

Not succumbing to fear is another lesson we can draw from this event. Only two of the ten, *Yehoshua ben Nun*, and *Calev ben Yefuneh*, stood their ground, and exhorted the people to rise above their crippling fears. One, *Yehoshua ben Nun*/Joshua, son of Nun, was Moshe's right hand man, and before the mission Moshe had changed his name from *Hoshea* to *Yehoshua* (Numbers 13:16). He added to his name the letter *yud*, which, with two of the other letters in Yehoshua's name, *heh* and *vav* meant he bore within his name, the powerful 'four letter Name of God' (*yud-heh-vav-heh*). This is a powerful antidote to fear. When David, armed only with a sling shot, faced a giant with armour, he said *"You come to me with a sword, with a spear and with a javelin. But I come to you in the Name of the LORD of hosts."* 1 Samuel 17:45.

*Calev ben Yefuneh*'s/Caleb's efforts to turn the people away from fearing the negative reports can be explained by God saying in 14:24, *"But My servant Caleb because he has a different spirit in him and followed me fully..."*

## Numbers 15
### Remembering That God Means What He Says

The beginning of this chapter shows that in spite of failure, God's promises stand. 'WHEN', not 'IF' *"... you come in...."* And so the instructions continue for their guaranteed future life, including details for ongoing cleansing from sin and failure along with the sombre warning of 'high-handed' sin for which that person would be cut off from the people with their guilt remaining, (Numbers 15:30-31). Hebrews 10:26 says, *"For if we sin wilfully after we have received the knowledge of the truth, there no longer remains a sacrifice for sins."* Breaking God's laws in a high-handed way is akin to putting oneself in the place of God and that is idolatry. The next passage is an example of this understanding.

Numbers 15:32-36 is an example of swift and dramatic judgement being enacted on someone breaking God's clear instructions. Romans 6:22-23 NLT makes it clear that there are consequences to sin. *"But now you are free from the power of sin and have become slaves of God. Now you do those things that lead to holiness and result in eternal life. For the wages of sin is death, but the free gift of God is eternal life through Christ Jesus our Lord."* In our passage in Numbers, someone was deliberately disobeying the sanctity of Shabbat by gathering sticks. We have seen in Exodus and other places that God had spelt out the rules regarding the Seventh Day, and the punishment for disobeying them. There were many instances of Sabbath desecration that followed after this account without necessarily the dramatic public consequences as in this case. But this was a first and God made it clear that the Sabbath, the Seventh Day, both His gift of it to the Jewish people and its strict rules, were extremely important and was not to be treated lightly. This is because the picture that God embedded in it was a precious one as explained before in the '*The Elegance of Exodus*', relating to Hebrews 4:9-10.

Following this transgression and the seeming failure to realise that God's commandments are meant to be obeyed, they were to have a constant visual reminder and in Numbers 15:37-41, a new instruction was issued. Something was to be added to their garments.

God used customs familiar to ancient peoples. In this example a fringe (tassels) on a hem told of the wearer's authority. The more tassels, the more authority. It was usually the nobility who wore them and who displayed the colour blue especially, which in ancient times was very expensive.

That threads were tied together to form tassels is derived from Deuteronomy 22:12 where a different Hebrew word is used, *"You shall make yourself tassels [Hebrew – gedil/twisted threads], on the four corners of your garment with which you cover yourself."*

As well as giving His people something visual to remind them of all the commandments, these tassels bestowed authority on them and spoke of royal heritage. The tassels also meant the wearer carried a symbol of the priesthood which endorsed him as being part of a priestly nation, Exodus 19:6, *"And you shall be to Me a kingdom of priests and a holy nation."* As it was difficult to dye linen the material most people wore, scholars therefore assume that the blue thread must have been wool. But it was prohibited in the Torah to wear cloth containing both wool and linen, except for the priests' garments. So having a wool tassel on a linen garment represented a priestly garment. Another connection to the priesthood is that the word fringe/'*tzitzit*', is a derivative of '*tzit*', which was the name of the gold band which the priests wore on their turbans, see Exodus 28:36, "*You shall also make a plate/tzit of pure gold…*"

The fringes or tassels, known as t*zitziot* in Hebrew (plural of tzitzit), were outward symbols of the 613 commandments of God, so a tradition developed for each tassel to comprise of eight strings with five knots. Using a process known as *Gematria*[39], Aish.com explains why:

'The eight strings and five knots are a physical representation of the Torah's 613 mitzvahs/commandments. It works like this: Each letter in the Hebrew alphabet has a corresponding numerical value (*gematria*). The numerical values of the five letters that comprise the Hebrew word *tzitzit* add up to 600. Add the eight strings and five knots of each tassel, and the total is 613'.

Many Jews today wear a tunic under their outer clothing with the tzitziot hanging from the four corners and visible outside their other garments. Otherwise, tzitziot hang from the *tallit/* prayer shawl which they don for prayer.

The Greek word that the King James translators rendered 'hem' in the New Testament is *kraspedon*. This is the same word that is used three times in Numbers 15:37-41 in the Septuagint, the

---

[39] Gematria is a numerological system by which Hebrew letters correspond to numbers. One can then calculate the numerical value of a word by adding together the values of each letter in it. In the realm of biblical interpretation, commentators base an argument on numerological equivalence of words. If a word's numerical value equals that of another word, a commentator might draw a connection between these two words and the verses in which they appear and use this to prove larger conceptual conclusions. (My Jewish Learning)

ancient Greek translation of the Hebrew Scriptures, to translate tzitzit. Therefore, in Luke 8:43-44, where it may read, "... *touched the border or hem – <u>kraspedon -</u> of his garment...*" the woman rendered unclean by her constant flow of menstrual blood according to Leviticus 15:25, actually took hold of Yeshua's tzitzit. A bold and desperate measure! Touching a male was bad enough in her unclean state, but taking hold of that holy part of his garment was a huge act of faith, one for which she received healing and Yeshua's commendation, Luke 8:48, "*And He said to her, "Daughter, be of good cheer, your faith has made you well. Go in peace."* Along with other cultural traditions to do with fringes on a hem, taking hold of them while requesting something meant the person could not refuse.

The word for corners from which the ritual tassels hung is *kanaf* which also means wings. (Psalm 57:1 written by David, "*...for my soul trusts in You: yes, in the shadow of Your **wings** will I make my refuge...*") At the end of 'Gems from Genesis' we looked more deeply at that aspect of this beautiful outward symbol. Tzitzit is also an uncommon word for wings used once in the Bible in Jeremiah 48:9, "*Give <u>wings/tzit</u> to Moab...*"

Before we leave this topic, consider Numbers15:39, "*And you shall have the tassel, that you may look upon it and remember all the commandments of the LORD and do them, and that you may not follow the harlotry to which your own heart and your own eyes are inclined.*" This verse can be connected to Proverbs 7 which is a warning against being 'led astray'. Proverbs 7:21-27 "*With her enticing speech she caused him to yield, With her flattering lips she seduced him. Immediately he went after her, as an ox goes to the slaughter, Or as a fool to the correction of the stocks, Till an arrow struck his liver. As a bird hastens to the snare, He did not know it would cost his life. Now therefore, listen to me, my children; Pay attention to the words of my mouth: Do not let your heart turn aside to her ways, Do not stray into her paths; For she has cast down many wounded, And all who were slain by her were strong men. Her house is the way to hell, Descending to the chambers of death."*

This passage in Proverbs is talking of situations of a sexual nature but I believe it means a lot more than that particular warning. It speaks of <u>any</u> distractions that lure us away from our true purpose, the things that our weak nature may be drawn to causing us to be unfaithful to God. *"But each one is tempted when he is drawn away by his own desires and enticed,"* agrees James 1:14.

The tzitziot reminded them of who they were. As non-Jews we don't wear them but perhaps the advice in Proverbs 7:3b to the young man to write the wise words on his heart is a help. As in Psalm 119:11, *"Your word I have hidden in my heart, That I might not sin against You."* And from Colossians 3:2, *"Set your mind on the things above, not on the things that are on earth."*

## Numbers 16-18
## The Danger of Resenting God's Choices

These three chapters are one account of a serious challenge to the spiritual and national leadership of God's anointed leaders. We saw in the earlier chapters that God was drawing boundaries, giving everyone their location in the camp of Israel, their functions, their roles. Some had more elevated positions than others. It is God who raises up and puts down. He does the choosing. However, Korah who was the first cousin of Moshe and Aaron, along with Datan and Aviram of the tribe of Reuben, elevated themselves by 'rising up' against Moshe and Aaron in a threatening manner, (Numbers 16:2). Was Korah jealous of the high priest's position? His clan had a most holy and responsible position, (Numbers 4:15 & 7:9), that of carrying the Ark of the Covenant from the Holy of Holies and handling other sanctuary items. In Numbers 16:3, their perception of "...*all the congregation is holy...*" was based perhaps on the chosen status of the whole nation, or the fact that now they all wore a special item, the tzitziot, and it was this outward symbol that made holiness. They were yet to learn that holiness was evidenced in actions and in behaviour which came from a right heart and rebelling against God's placement was not an act of a holy people. Paul rebukes the Believers in Corinth for a similar failing, "*For you are still controlled by your sinful nature. You are jealous of one another and quarrel with each other. Doesn't that prove you are controlled by your sinful nature? Aren't you living like people of the world?*" 1 Corinthians 3:3 NLT.

Korah desired Aaron's place but Datan and Aviram desired Moshe's leadership position. They were of the Tribe of Reuben, the firstborn of Yakov's twelve sons who had lost his privileged firstborn position by sleeping with his father's concubine. Because of this disgrace, his father bypassed him and gave his firstborn rights to Judah. Perhaps the bitterness had been passed down the generations. We know that the poison of bitterness can indeed infect succeeding generations. They also showed contempt for someone appointed by God. In Numbers 16:28

Moshe could say he had not been working within his own will but only in the calling and will of God. Something we also need to be sure of at all times so we can also stand against accusations of presumption on our part. There may be times that challenges are a way of getting us back on track, but in this case, they were false and Moshe stood against them, Numbers 16:15.

Again, in this rebellion there was a looking back, seeing the old life back in Egypt but without the oppression and the chains and slavery, but rather, as a place that even compared with God's Promised Land! It was in fact a blasphemous statement and comes so soon after the spies' bad report and its disastrous consequences in chapters 13 and 14. They had not learned their lesson. The dramatic events of 16:32 and 35 which followed were not for the honour of Moshe but for the Word of the LORD.

This is a good time to note that the children of Korah did not perish (Numbers 26:11) and his descendants were writers of psalms, for example Psalms 42-49. What his children probably witnessed may have influenced them to be on the side of God! Our heritage, which may not be a Godly one, does not stop us from serving a holy God.

In Numbers 16:4-11, Moshe gave them a test. They aspired to the priesthood, 16:9-10, so let them present incense before the LORD, an act of worship that was reserved for the priests alone, and see if the LORD accepts their incense pan.

(Numbers 4:16 *"The appointed duty of Eleazar the son of Aaron the priest is the oil for the light, <u>the sweet incense,</u>*

*the daily grain offering, the anointing oil, the oversight of all the tabernacle, of all that is in it, with the sanctuary and its furnishings.*")

The test in 16:35 was decisive and dramatic. Fire consumed the men who aspired to a calling not theirs, and the hammered and remoulded fire pans would forever remain a warning as Moshe said in 16:40 "*...to be a memorial to the children of Israel that no outsider, who is not a descendant of Aaron, should come near to offer incense before the LORD, that he might not become like Korah and his companions...*"

Many of the congregation though blamed Moses and Aaron and in 16:41 their attitude became threatening until God intervened. The going gets tough at times and weariness can bring discontent, something Paul recognised when he exhorted in 2 Thessalonians 3:13 KJV, "*...be not weary in well doing...*" The people decided that things were definitely not working out as they were supposed to - of course - as a result of their own disobedience and fear, but their challenge to God's anointed leadership was treated extremely seriously by God. The rebellious spirit that had found fertile ground could end in destroying the redemptive plans that God was unfolding through the new nation. Korah had made himself a spokesperson for the people and made it sound as if he was their champion. But those who listened made a dreadful mistake. More than ever in this day of deceptions, when part truths can be mixed with false claims, we need to stand on God's Word and be very careful whose voice we heed. 2 Peter 3:17 says "*...beware lest you also fall from your own steadfastness, being led away with the error of the wicked...*"

In chapter 17 of Numbers, the spiritual leadership was settled once and for all by God demonstrating that the role of the high priest was connected to resurrection power. A connection that would be fulfilled in a wonderful way through 'The High Priest', to whom Aaron and his sons after him were pointing. Twelve dead 'sticks/rods', were placed before the LORD, each one representing leadership because a man's rod, or staff/*mata*, was a symbol of authority. One of them budded, blossomed and produced ripe almonds, 17:8. Life from death! We learnt something of the symbolism of the almond tree in chapter 8. In that case, it was a picture of God keeping His word no matter how bleak the circumstances. In the case of Aaron's rod, it was the authority and power He had bestowed on the high priest along with the uniqueness of that role. Note that the lampstand/ menorah which was carved in the likeness of an almond tree is a light in the darkness, a symbol of hope, and a representation of power and authority. No wonder that in Revelation 1:12-13, the resurrected and glorified Messiah appeared in the *"midst of the lampstands."*

Numbers 17:12-13 expresses the fear which gripped the people as they witnessed a further demonstration of God's dramatic judgements.

However, throughout chapter 18 there is affirmation that if they keep within the boundaries God has drawn, they are protected from such severe discipline. As well as the separate roles and functions that God had established in this chapter (Numbers 18), He now emphasizes those distinctions, and again the responsibilities and benefits are spelt out.

When the Torah emphasizes or repeats details, we need to ask why? What is so important here? I believe a very important principle was being established. There is no room for jealousy! It is a principle that was made clear to the new Gentile Believers in Messiah. 1 Corinthians 12:4-6, *"There are diversities of gifts but the same Spirit. There are differences of ministries but the same Lord. And there are diversities of activities but the same God who works all in all."*

And one of the warnings against jealousy in the Body of Messiah in the New Testament is from James 3:14, *"But if you have bitter envy and self-seeking in your hearts, do not boast and lie against the truth."*

## Numbers 19
## The Cost of Cleansing

Chapter 19 is the beginning of a weekly Torah Portion which is called *Chukat*. As explained before, the portions have been named, usually, by a word which begins or is near the beginning of the passage. The shorter form of 'chukat', *'chok'*, is in verse 2 and is translated 'statute' or 'ordinance'. It is one of several words to describe God's directives along with 'commandment', 'precept', or 'judgement'. *Chok* though is a strong word and often associated with a commandment for which the reason is not understood. The ritual of the Red Heifer is such a one, and Jewish scholars accept from this passage that there are things we are not expected to understand completely, but that the main thing is that we obey regardless. After all, 1 Corinthians 13:9 tells us that *"we know in part..."* If we could understand everything we would be equal to God, something that man, beginning with Adam has often aspired to. Obeying and trusting even that which is beyond our human intellect demonstrates humility. Avraham, obeying the command to sacrifice his son, displayed such obedience by following an instruction that made no logical sense.

We can attempt to see what picture God has for us here by looking at some of the symbolism interwoven into the ritual regarding the Red Heifer. Firstly, we notice a paradox - that which purifies the unclean person, defiles the agent performing the ritual. It purifies the impure and at the same time, renders the pure, impure. Therefore, this ritual required compassion on the part of the priest to go through all that was required of him. His love for his people resulted in his impurity and inconvenience in needing to become ritually clean again.

This is a good place to note something! That is, that Israel which brought a purifying light to the nations has been despised by many of those nations.

Continuing with the symbolism, we see that the lofty cedar of Lebanon, symbolic of pride, and the lowly hyssop, symbolic of humility, are two of the items that were required in the healing of the leper. A cleansing from defilement requires pride to be replaced by humility. The scarlet thread included with the cedar and hyssop is symbolic of sin, bringing to mind Isaiah 1:18, *"...Though your sins are like scarlet, they shall be as white as snow; though they are red like crimson, they shall be as wool."*

He who was without sin became sin we are told in 2 Corinthians 5:21, and Hebrews 9:13 says, *"If the blood of goats and bulls and the ashes of a heifer sprinkling those who have been defiled, sanctifies for the purifying of the flesh, how much more the blood of Christ."*

The heifer was not sacrificed on the bronze altar but outside the camp, on the Mount of Olives. Therefore, I believe this is the most likely place where Yeshua was crucified. *"Jesus also, that He might sanctify the people with His own blood, suffered outside the gate. Therefore, let us go forth to Him, outside the camp, bearing His reproach."* Hebrews 13:12-13. The Mount of Olives is also the only location that was in direct line to the Holy of Holies, in front of which all acceptable sacrifices were made.

As a matter of interest, should the temple be rebuilt, Judaism requires the ashes of a red heifer for purifying purposes in order to recommence temple rituals. The search for a perfect red heifer has been going on for some time. A possible red heifer is disqualified should there be anywhere on its body, two non-red hairs close to each other or three non-red hairs far apart or any other kind of blemish.

**The Defilement of Death**

From Numbers 19:11 to the end, is a most important principle, one we came across in chapter 5. Contact with death causes defilement and needs cleansing prescribed by God. One must not associate if possible, with that which brings 'death' rather than 'life'. Just as the kashrut laws taught the Jewish people not to eat the meat of animals that fed on carcasses, (death), so we need to feed our minds and spirits on that which nourishes. Psalm 101:3 has good advice for today's visual and digital world, *"I will set nothing wicked before my eyes."*

## Numbers 20
## It's Not About Us

The Torah does not hide the faults of great men, no matter what their status. And here we see Moshe, after all these years of coping with a complaining, ungrateful people, display anger. We may easily feel sympathy with Moshe for his exasperation, and wonder at the harsh punishment that followed: not to go into the Promised Land, so near! However, to whom much is given much shall be required. More was expected of him than the people he served. Many of the Jewish sages agree that by claiming that it was him and Aaron bringing forth the miracle, 20:10, he had desecrated God's name, *chillul Hashem* as it is called in Hebrew. Unguarded moments can cause us to bring shame on God's name too and undo all that's gone before. Both the Tanach [40] and New Testament give plenty of warnings about not giving in to anger.

I believe too that Moshe spoiled the picture that God intended for us in the 'water from the rock' scenario which is why it resulted in his severe punishment. In 1 Corinthians 10:4, Paul

---

[40] The name of the Bible, that is the 'Old Testament', in Judaism. It is an acrostic of the three sections: Torah, Nasim/Prophets, Chotvim/Writings.

quotes a *midrash*[41] from the Oral Law which said the rock followed them. He interpreted it to mean it was a picture of Messiah. *"For they drank of that spiritual Rock that followed them, and that Rock was Messiah."* The first time water flowed from the rock, Moshe had been told to strike the rock: Exodus 17:6, *"Behold, I will stand before you there on the rock in Horeb; and you shall strike the rock, and water will come out of it, that the people may drink. And Moses did so in the sight of the elders of Israel."* The second time here in this chapter, Numbers 20:8, Moshe was told to speak to the rock.

And this was the picture - Messiah was 'struck' once, and since then one only has to ask to receive life-giving spiritual water as John 7:37-38 says, *"On the last day, that great day of the feast, Jesus stood and cried out, saying, 'If anyone thirsts, let him come to Me and drink. He who believes in Me, as the Scripture has said, out of his heart will flow rivers of living water'."*

Note that the water stopped flowing after Miriam's death, Numbers 20:1-2. Jewish commentators say it was connected to her death. Some think it was because there was not the proper amount of grieving for such a special person, (compare 20:29 when Aaron died). After all, her death is recorded in quite an emotionless way. She had watched over baby brother Moshe in the waters of the Nile and led the people in praise after crossing the Sea of Reeds. Consequently she did have a connection with water. However, we can merely note that in spite of her lapse in chapter12, she is a role model of faith that we can follow.

---

[41] A very simple explanation of Midrash is that it is a commentary and can include stories to illustrate the meaning of a Biblical text.

## To Stand or not Stand, with Israel

In 20:14-21, Israel approaches Edom, descendants of Yakov's brother, Esau/*Esav*, asking for a favour. Edom refuses to help and begins a sad pattern throughout the history of nations that have a connection to Israel through shared values, or beneficiaries of Israel's knowledge, or simply owing a debt for the Biblical values on which their country may have been founded. These nations have also refused to help Israel in time of need. Checking facts about the conflicts that the modern State has endured with hostile neighbours including its fight for survival in the War of Independence, will show that desperately needed support from its allies in the West during those times was mostly refused or delayed.

Later in Deuteronomy other nations are named that Israel is forbidden to harm because of a relationship connection. Therefore, Israel did well to turn away in this case. There are times to simply walk away from those who reject all overtures of friendship, rather than allowing resentment to develop and possibly result in actions that are against God's instructions.

## Numbers 21
### Choose Judgement or Choose Healing.

Death continues to be a theme in these last two chapters because in chapter 20:24-29, Aaron dies and the high priestly garments, so rich in significance, are transferred to his son, Eleazar.

Unbelievably the people following a military victory in Numbers 21:1-3 continue to complain, (21:4-5). Perhaps they were fed up at having to backtrack because of not being able to go through Edom's territory, and probably there were many who could not see why they simply could not have gone through with force. So they accused not only Moshe (as they had done in the past), but also God, calling His supernaturally provided food worthless. In response, the LORD sent fiery serpents, causing many deaths. In Jewish writings (Targum Yerushalim) it is said that God declared from Heaven, 'the serpent did not complain of its food, dust, (Genesis 3:14), but My people complain of manna – it will punish those who slander God'.

In John 3:14, Yeshua compared the serpent lifted up, to him being lifted up, *"And as Moses lifted up the serpent in the wilderness, even so must the Son of man be lifted up."* What is the connection? In Numbers 21:8-9 by looking in obedience at that which brought judgement, the people received healing. Obedience to what seemed an illogical thing to do was required. They had to look up at an 'object' for healing which was the same object that represented God's judgement. And we should note here that the bronze serpent was made of the same material as the bronze altar where sin was also 'judged' through the innocent life that was sacrificed on it. Most of the world disdains the provision and grace of God as illogical, not realizing that this leads to eternal separation from Him.

It is worth noting that the word translated as fiery, is *saraph*. This is the same word used for the seraphim who wait on God around his throne, see Isaiah 6:2.

Supernatural manifestations of heavenly things are most often associated with fire such as the chariots of fire seen by Elisha and his servant in 2 Kings 6:17b: "*And behold, the mountain was full of horses and <u>chariots of fire</u> all around Elisha.*" On Mt Sinai in Exodus 19:18: "*...the LORD descended upon it in <u>fire...</u>*" and in the 'Covenant of the Halves' in Genesis 15:17, "*And it came to pass, when the sun went down and it was dark, that behold, there appeared a <u>smoking oven and a burning torch</u> that passed between those pieces.*"

## Victory over Giants

Israel had no thought of attacking nations on the way to Canaan and asked to pass through peacefully. However, they did have permission from the LORD to fight some nations and He did give them victory. Sihon was a formidable foe as we read in this chapter. And Og was part of the giant race which had struck fear into Israel a generation before, descendants of the *Nephilim*, the offspring of the fallen angels and human women. Perhaps the genes were carried in a daughter in law of Noah in order for some giants to have survived the Flood. No one really knows. Sihon and Og and the Israelites' defeat of them, 21:23-24 and 21:33-35, are referred to several times in the Torah and later scriptures, and their influence is still remembered much later in Israelite history as 1 Kings 4:19 shows, when needing to identify the location of various leaders, "*Geber the son of Uri was in the country of Gilead, in the country of <u>Sihon</u> king of the Amorites, and of <u>Og</u> king of Bashan; and he was the only governor which was in the land.*"

## Numbers 22
## Where Does the Heart Lie?

Because the Israelites had defeated the Amorites in an unprovoked battle, and because Moab/*Moav* had relied on the Amorites for protection, Balak, Moav's King, panicked even though according to Deuteronomy 2:9 Israel was not going to attack them. Too scared to take them on militarily, Balak hired a mysterious pagan sorcerer, Balaam/*B'laam*, who obviously had a well-known reputation for being able to bring blessings or curses on people through his words, and who also knew of the God of Israel and His power. Actually in the request to B'laam to curse those whom he perceived as enemies, Balak used a word which was a milder form of curse, *arar* in Numbers 22:6, but in verse 11 when B'laam sought the LORD for help he used another word for curse *kavav* which was much stronger.

There are other details in this story, especially in the original Hebrew, that bring out the full drama and cultural background and the manipulation of this greedy prophet. We will look at two aspects. One explains an apparent changing of God's mind. In verses 12 and 20, He first instructs B'laam not to go with the princes of Balak, then, in verse 21 says he can go, but then punishes him for doing so. Two small Hebrew words are translated 'with' in English. However, they each have a different shade of meaning. '*Eem*' means being <u>with</u> someone in spirit, in unity. '*Et*' is like sharing a seat with a stranger on a bus. You are <u>with</u> someone, but only in proximity not emotionally.

B'laam was told by God in verse 20 he could go 'with/*et*' them but in verse 21, B'laam went 'with/*eem*' them. He was one in spirit with those wanting to destroy the people of God. However, as God proved with the donkey, He could control mouths!

The other aspect about B'laam was his greed and Jude 1:11 speaking of ungodly men warns, *"Woe to them! For they have gone in the way of Cain, have run greedily in the <u>error of Balaam</u> for profit, and perished in the rebellion of Korah."* And 2 Peter 2:15 makes reference to his greedy nature and his hope of material reward, *"They have forsaken the right way and gone astray, following the <u>way of Balaam</u> the son of Beor, who loved the wages of unrighteousness."*

Numbers 22:18 may sound pious but it was a typical Middle Eastern way of angling for more payment. The exchange between Abraham and the Hittite, Ephron in Genesis 23:7-16 when Abraham wanted to buy land to bury Sarah is similar. Especially in verse 11 when it seems as if Ephron would give the land away, *"No my lord, hear me, I give you the field and the cave that is in it…"* But it was only a prelude to bargaining.

## Numbers 23 & 24
## God Turns What is Meant for Evil into Blessings

However, the words that B'laam spoke were words of blessing not cursing. In fact, some of his words are included in formal Jewish prayers. Because we know they are words from God, we can read and meditate on some of the inspiring concepts and prophecies that came out of his mouth concerning God's beloved nation. We can also take hold of those concepts for ourselves knowing that those whom God calls His own are beloved, protected, and His promises for them are brought to pass.

## Numbers 25
## There are Different Tactics to Defeat the People of God

B'laam though was not finished. He gave the king of Moav some advice which Numbers 31:16 indicates was to 'lure them with pleasures, introduce them to a lifestyle that was forbidden to them by the laws of a holy God'. Revelation 2:14 confirms this, *"But I have a few things against you, because you have there those who hold the doctrine of Balaam, who taught Balak to put a stumbling block before the children of Israel, to eat things sacrificed to idols, and to commit sexual immorality."*

Many succumbed to the perverted ways of paying homage to the idol *'Peor'*. But not all, as verse 6 indicates. Some were weeping before the *mishkan,* the tabernacle. The terrible state of affairs hit a sad low when a son of an Israelite community leader and the daughter of a Midianite leader blatantly indulged in a sex act in front of the congregation. The LORD warned Moshe to act quickly to avoid judgement and indeed a plague broke out. Phinehas/*Pinchas*, a priest, acted with zeal.

The disgusting so-called worship of Peor also included defecating in front of the idol. In other words, what comes naturally, do! Do not worry about cultural or moral restraints. No need for self-discipline and acting within the parameter for the greater good. A mindset that is sadly apparent in the morality of today's Western nations. Pinchas' action was harsh and decisive and would have been criticized by the politically correct that sees human freedoms allowable no matter the effect on others. Paul may have acted 'politically incorrectly' too in 1 Corinthians 5:1-5 when in speaking of a grievous sin being tolerated by the community he said in verse 5, "*...deliver such a one to Satan for the destruction of the flesh that his spirit maybe saved in the day of the Lord Jesus.*"

Actually Pinchas' action, because it involved bloodshed, should have disqualified him from the priesthood. But he was prepared to forfeit his status in order to restore the fellowship between the people and their God. However, the priesthood was guaranteed to his descendants, Numbers 25:13; and Psalm 106:28-31 relates the account and says in verse 31, his act of faith and courage "*was accounted to him for righteousness*" which are the same words said regarding the faith of Abraham in Genesis 15:6 and quoted in Romans 4:3.

In Numbers 25:10-13, God made it clear Pinchas had acted correctly and granted him protection by giving him a 'covenant of peace'/*brit shalom*. This designation is used again in Ezekiel 37: 26 in relation to Messiah's reign, "*Moreover I will make a <u>covenant of peace [brit shalom]</u> with them, and it shall be an everlasting covenant with them...*" What a gift! Peace with God! Romans 5:1 says that we have a *brit shalom*/'peace with God' through the Messiah. His atoning actions like Pinchas, protect us from the wrath of God and that's why he could say in John 14:27, "*...My peace/shalom I give to you...*"

Not only were the Israelites punished, but God decreed that the Midianites would also be punished and it would be at the hand of the Israelites, (Numbers 25:16-18). God takes seriously the matter of turning someone away from their faith in Him. Luke 17:1-2 NIV recounts these serious words of Yeshua, *"Jesus said to his disciples: 'Things that cause people to stumble are bound to come, but woe to anyone through whom they come. It would be better for them to be thrown into the sea with a millstone tied around their neck than to cause one of these little ones to stumble'."* I believe 'little ones' can mean those young in the ways of following God.

## Numbers 26
## A New Beginning

The numbering for which this book received its English name continues by way of another census, now 38 years on. It takes place as they stand on the brink of finally entering the Promised Land. Apart from Calev and Yehoshua the first generation had died. But God is the God of new beginnings, of second chances, of being 'born again' and becoming a 'new creation'. See 2 Corinthians 5:17 HNV, *"Therefore, if anyone is in Messiah, he is a new creation; old things have passed away; behold, all things have become new."*

## Numbers 27
## When to Claim and not Claim Rights

In Numbers 27:1-4, Zelophehad's fatherless daughters brought their case to the representative of their heavenly Father. In line with always seeking the LORD's directions for the nation,

Moshe brought this new situation to Him and yes, the girls' rights were there all the time for them, (27:5-11), they just needed to claim them. Later, in Joshua 17:3-4 they reminded Yehoshua and Eleazer the High Priest of those rights when the land was being allotted, and received their rightful inheritance.

Moshe continues to provide a role model for God's people and certainly for leaders, (27:12-17). In spite of his huge disappointment at not being the one to lead the people over the border, his thought was immediately for the people's well-being without him, and God assures him that Yehoshua will be the one to lead the people. Moshe publicly lays hands on Yehoshua to ordain him as leader in 27:22-23. At this point I think this explanation from Tom Bradford, www.torahclass.com is worth reading:

'Yehoshua was to be a military leader of Israel not a mediator. When Moses needed answers from the LORD, or the LORD wanted to tell Moses something, He made direct communication with Moses. This would not usually be so with Yehoshua. Yehoshua was NOT going to be the new mediator of Israel. I have mentioned before that the LORD has in all of history supplied but TWO mediators, and two only. And that is all there ever will be. Moses was the first, Yeshua the second. Neither had a successor. Oh some of their duties were assigned; Yehoshua was to rule over, care for and lead Israel; and we Believers are to spread the Good News and demonstrate Christ's sacrificial love. But we are not the replacement mediators for Jesus, we are but His disciples. So with the coming death of Moses it would be around 12 centuries before the Father would provide a new and better mediator than Moses. And now that Yeshua is dead and risen, there will not ever be another. When He comes again, it will not be as mediator, but as the Kinsman Redeemer'.

# Numbers 28
# Daily Dedication

In verses 1-15, there are details which deal with the daily, and other regular times of offerings. I want to draw attention to a few of those details. The phrase 'pleasing', or 'sweet aroma to the LORD' generally follows mention of each burnt offering. I will repeat some teaching from chapters 1-7: 'Provision of Pardon' in *'Lessons from Leviticus'*, because it is an important principle:

'The Burnt Offering' is called in Hebrew the *Oleh* offering, meaning 'to rise up' because it was totally consumed on the altar, and its aroma rose up to God. See Genesis 8:20,21 and Exodus 29:18. This offering represents total dedication. Ephesians 5:2 says, *"...as Christ has also loved us and given himself for us, an offering and a sacrifice to God for a sweet smelling aroma."* There was an aspect of Yeshua's sacrifice that was for the Father alone. The Hebrew phrase *re'ach nicho'ach l'adonai - "a pleasing fragrance to the LORD"* is used over 40 times in the Torah. We know it was not the smell of roast lamb that pleased the LORD, but a form of satisfying joy for Him when He saw the dedication, the commitment and the genuine heart, expressed through the offering of the worshipper'.

Numbers 28:11 includes the words - 'beginnings of your months' - in the instructions concerning sacrifices and offerings. The beginning, or new month is marked by the new moon. It was important to know when the months began because this was the way of keeping track of time and seasons and knowing the right days on which the various celebrations fell. *"He appointed the moon for seasons..."* says Psalm 104:19, 'seasons' being the translation of *'mo'adim'* - appointments. Each new Hebrew month is still marked by the Jewish people today with special praise and prayers and sometimes commemorative meals. God was particular about His people observing and controlling time. After all, as we've seen, He gave them special dates which they are to set aside, including the weekly one, in order to meet with Him. While we Believers out of the nations do not have to observe the Jewish calendar (though enjoying and honouring those dates can be a tremendous blessing), a clear principle is embedded in its establishment. It is that God has given us a life to be lived to the fullest and lived according to His personal timetable that He has set for our lives in order for us to know the most satisfaction. Psalm 90:12 says, *"So teach us to number our days, that we may gain a heart of wisdom."*

## Numbers 28 cont. & 29
## God's Appointment Calendar

Chapter 28:16 through to 29:40 deals with the various festivals which God had instructed His people to keep. As we have looked at these special appointments with the LORD before, we will note just a few things. In 28:16-17 we can see that there are actually two festivals listed here: Passover and the Feast of Unleavened Bread. Passover/*Pesach* is on the 14th day of the First Month which, since the Babylonian Exile, has been called *Nisan,* but in the Torah is called *Aviv.* Then the day after, on the 15th day the seven day Feast of Unleavened Bread/ *Hag HaMatzot* begins. *Pesach* celebrates the redemption from bondage and during *Hag HaMatzot* no leaven/*hametz* which represents a corrupting influence, is eaten. Here is a wonderful clear picture, Pesach establishes that God's part is to redeem His people; Hag HaMatzot, that our part is to rid ourselves of that which corrupts, or puffs up.

The next festival, fifty days later, is the celebration called the Feast of Weeks/*Shavuot*, which was the beginning of the main harvest, the tangible result of the blessings of God in their lives which followed their obedient walk with Him.

The following festival in 29:1 called 'a day of blowing'/*Yom Tru'ah,* is declared on the first day of the seventh month, *Tishrei.* We have also looked at this festival before, but can note here that although the Hebrew does not say which instrument is to be blown, and 'trumpets' has been added in the English, it is understood that it is a rams horn/*shofar.* Exodus 2:23-24 says, *"...then the children of Israel groaned because of the bondage, and they cried out; and their cry came up to God because of the bondage. So God heard their groaning..."* The groaning, or sighing, that God heard was a prayer, but not with words, Jewish commentators say. And the sound of the shofar, also sounded before the Day of Atonement, is like that wordless cry to God. There are times when we do not have words, only deep longings that cannot be expressed. Even creation is waiting for restoration from the Creator at the time when God's reign and glory will be manifest on earth. Romans 8:21-22, *"...because the creation itself also will be delivered from the bondage of corruption into the glorious liberty of the children of God. For we know that the whole creation groans and labours with birth pangs together until now."* But not only the creation, 8:23, *"... but we also who have the firstfruits of the Spirit, even we ourselves groan within ourselves, eagerly waiting for the adoption, the redemption of our body."*

Another significant instruction regarding these appointment days, is related to the Feast of Tabernacles/*Sukkot*, 29:12. This joyous time comes five days after the Day of Atonement/*Yom Kippur*, Numbers 29:7-11. And just as that intense and awe inspiring day points toward <u>The</u> Judgement Day, so the happy festival of *Sukkot* points towards a Day hinted at in Revelation 21:3-4, *"...Behold, the tabernacle of God is with men, and He will dwell with them, and they shall be His people. God Himself will be with them and be their God. And God will wipe away every tear from their eyes..."* Sukkot, say the Rabbis, is Messianic – all the children of man will one day dwell under the tabernacle of one Heavenly Father. Therefore, an important instruction to take note of is the number of sacrifices which, the Rabbis say, were made on behalf of the Gentiles. Numbers 29:13 says to sacrifice 13 bulls on the first day, and the verses go through each day reducing that number by one. By the end of the seventh day, the total number adds up to 70 bulls - one bull for each of the 70 nations. As mentioned in *'Gems from Genesis'*, the number of nations is 70 because Deuteronomy 32:8b says, *"He set the boundaries of the peoples according to the number of the children of Israel."* And 70 was the number of Jacob's family when they went into Egypt. Genesis 46:27b, *"All the persons of the house of Jacob who went to Egypt were seventy."* At the time when God was leading His people into the Promised Land, and instructing them how He wanted them to live as set apart people, the majority of those in the nations had no knowledge or interest in God. Idolatry separated them from their Creator, so Israel sacrificed on their behalf during the Festival of Sukkot. This was in line with Israel's calling to be a channel of redemption to the nations. Through them, God would reveal the fullness of His redemptive plan.

## Numbers 30
## Commitment is a Serious Matter

Again, as in Leviticus 27, we see just how seriously the LORD views vows or oaths made to Him. Yeshua warned in Matthew 5:37, *"But let your 'Yes' be 'Yes,' and your 'No,' be 'No.' For whatever is more than these is from the evil one."*

And so did James 5:12, *"But above all, my brethren, do not swear, either by heaven or by earth or with any other oath. But let your 'Yes' be 'Yes', and your 'No,' be 'No', lest you fall into judgment."*

Moshe conveyed the commandment of the LORD concerning this matter of vows to the heads of the tribes. It was such a serious matter that it was considered the spiritual responsibility of the leaders to ensure the obligations were adhered to. As a community, it was important that individual commitment was not to be taken lightly or neglected. This is a good reminder for us that our spiritual life is not to be lived in isolation. The emphasis on individuality in today's Christian thinking was not the principle that God laid down in Torah, and the New Testament endorses the fact that the people of God should operate as a community and share collective responsibility for each other.

Responsibility also rested on the men of the household to ensure that daughters or wives did not put themselves in positions deserving judgement because of careless vows. This is not to be thought of as submission of women, but of putting the responsibility for the spiritual health of their households on men. Rather than take anything away from women, instead, this direction lifts that responsibility from their shoulders. In many Christian homes, it is often the woman who takes the lead for ensuring the family is attending a fellowship and praying with the children, whereas Ephesians 6:4 says clearly, *"And you, fathers, do not provoke your children to wrath, but bring them up in the training and admonition of the Lord."* Though Galatians 3:28 firmly asserts that male and female are one in Messiah as far as redemption is concerned, different roles are assumed. And dare we ask does God understand that women are sometimes ruled by emotion? By the way, if the man makes a mistake in annulling her vow, that is also on his head, (Numbers 30:15). He needs to be in a right place with God in order to make a judgement on behalf of someone else.

## Numbers 31
## Holy War

God's people were sometimes warned against going to war, and other times are instructed by the LORD to do so. Israel invariably suffered defeat when they engaged in battles which they were not told to undertake. When God directed them to fight their enemies, there was victory. *"Vengeance is mine"* says the LORD in Deuteronomy 32:35 and quoted in Romans 12:19. God is the righteous judge and He knows when vengeance is due. Note that in Numbers 31:1-2 God says to Moshe that vengeance on the Midianites was for the sake of, or on behalf of, the people. In verse 3, Moshe relates it to vengeance for the LORD. This is a lovely picture that is both an encouraging and a serious reminder that God and His people are bound together.

Their honour is His honour, their shame His too. He allies Himself with them.

Knowing something of the culture of the nations of that region at that time makes 31:17 a little easier to understand. Males were obliged to take vengeance for their fathers' deaths. In this case, their Midianite fathers had died at the hands of Israelites. Therefore, had the young males grown to adulthood they would one day turn on those responsible. Does this make the directive regarding so much bloodshed more palatable for our sensitive Western minds? Maybe not entirely, as we like to mould God in our image at times – actually, a form of idolatry! But firstly, we must always keep cultural context in mind and secondly, remember our understanding is finite.

The purpose of this Study though is to remember 'all scripture is for our instruction' and see what principle is embedded in this passage for us. There is a personal lesson for us throughout the Torah, the Prophets and into the New Testament, in which God's people are urged to be rid of corrupting influences and evil that can so easily attach themselves to our minds and find entrance into our hearts. *"Therefore, get rid of all moral filth and the evil that is so prevalent and humbly accept the word planted in you, which can save you."* James 1:21. Also, Jude 1:4-23 warned the early Church to be discerning and recognising those intent on harm, *"For certain men have crept in unnoticed, who long ago were marked out for this condemnation, ungodly men, who turn the grace of our God into lewdness and deny the only Lord God and our Lord Jesus Christ."* Jude 1:4

Other New Testament passages have similar warnings such as 2 Peter 2:1 and Titus 1:16. When appeasement and tolerance of ungodliness is mistaken for the love that Believers are certainly commanded to show, the Body of Messiah is no longer maintaining a holy walk before God.

Note in Numbers 31:19-26, following contact with death, the laws of purity were obeyed and included the water of purification which came from the ritual of the Red Heifer, (Numbers 19:9).

Chapter 31:25-54 is a scrupulous reckoning of the spoils of battle so it could be shared among those who fought and those who had to remain, with the LORD receiving His due. A principle endorsed by Paul in 1 Corinthians 9:8-11 NLT, *"For the law of Moses says, 'You must not muzzle an ox to keep it from eating as it treads out the grain.' Was God thinking only about oxen when he said this? Wasn't he actually speaking to us? Yes, it was written for us, so that the one who plows and the one who threshes the grain might both expect a share of the harvest."*

## Numbers 32 & 33
## Finishing the Journey

Most of chapter 32 deals with the request of the tribes of Gad and Reuven to settle on the east side of the Jordan. This area was outside the boundaries of the Promised Land, and Moshe gave a stern warning not to make the same mistake of the ten 'spies'. These two tribes could also discourage the community by not wanting to go into the Promised Land. Their intentions were resolved and promises secured to send their fighters to help the other tribes. Half of the tribe of Manasseh also settled on that side, Numbers 32:39, taking the land of the Amorites whom the Israelites had defeated.

In chapter 33, beginning with leaving Egypt, there is a recounting of the forty-two places to which they travelled in the 40 years of their journey. As we know, each move was dictated by the moving of the Cloud. When setting out to unknown territory, it's safer to closely follow the directions of God. Psalm 106 is also a summary of the history of their deliverance from slavery, their journey including the times they sinned against the LORD. *"Nevertheless He saved them for His Name's sake, that He might make His mighty power known."* Psalm 106:8. What love and what encouragement! He does not abandon His people but is ever ready to forgive.

## Numbers 34
### Keeping Within God's Boundaries

Events are moving towards entry into the Land of Israel. Moshe conveys from the LORD's directives, the borders of their tribal allocations within their homeland. We have already seen that God is a God of order including putting people and nations into the right positions. Acts 17:26, *"And He has made from one blood every nation of men to dwell on all the face of the earth, and has determined their pre-appointed times and the boundaries of their dwellings."*

This chapter is about the physical boundaries of Israel, but God had previously also set moral and ethical boundaries for

His people to live by through the Torah. Without boundaries, there is no structure, and when boundaries are removed there is vulnerability and confusion. Today results can sadly be seen within families and societies where children are brought up with no clearly defined and well-kept boundaries that place limits on behavioural and moral activities which harm themselves and others. In the list of curses that the Children of Israel recite on Mount Ebal, (Deuteronomy 27:17) one is, *"Cursed is the one who moves his neighbour's landmark..."* These words are speaking of the geographical boundaries of one's inheritance. But equally wrong are the decisions that remove proven boundaries of responsible conduct, and allow unfettered movement into the rights and lives of others.

## Numbers 35
## What Do We Make Our Refuge?

The Levites did not receive any tribal inheritance, but were to be given 48 cities with land around them, distributed within the tribal allotments. Of those cities, six had to be designated as Cities of Refuge/*miklat*. (By way of interest, modern Hebrew applies that word, *miklat*, to bomb shelters that are found in every public building and apartment block in Israel). The Cities of Refuge were places of protection for the person who caused an accidental death. According to tradition, the Avenger of Blood had every right to avenge the death of his relative. Justice demands revenge! *"...The soul that sins shall die."* (Ezekiel 18:4). *"Be sure of this: The wicked will not go unpunished, but those who are righteous will go free."* Proverbs 11:21 NIV. But Mercy awaits and offers refuge! A picture of God providing refuge, including the Cities of Refuge, is one that emerges through these five Books of Torah, also painted so beautifully many times by the psalmists; for example in Psalm 46:1, *"God is our refuge and strength, A very present help in trouble."*

And this same picture is used by the writer of Hebrews 6:18 NLT when he says, *"So God has given both his promise and his oath. These two things are unchangeable because it is impossible for God to lie. Therefore, we who have fled to him for refuge can have great confidence as we hold to the hope that lies before us."*

We can note another beautiful picture here: the wrong doer found release <u>after</u> the death of the high priest. We have seen several times during these Torah studies that there were various aspects of the role of high priest which pointed to <u>our</u> High Priest. Here is another in Numbers 35:25 - the death of the high priest had to occur to release the one worthy of punishment.

Another aspect at which we will look only briefly, is that the term generally translated as 'Avenger of Blood' is more correctly translated 'Redeemer of Blood' and can also be translated as 'Kinsman Redeemer'. It was one of the duties of the Kinsman Redeemer to bring justice. We were introduced to the Kinsman Redeemer in Leviticus 25:25 in a more benign context and that role is displayed in the lovely story of Ruth in the Book of Ruth. Here in Numbers 35:24-28 we see him in a role that is exacting justice.

Revelation 19:11-16 also shows the One we call Kinsman Redeemer in this role. Verse 15, *"...He himself treads the*

*winepress of the fierceness and wrath of Almighty God.*" There
is an attribute of God which is terrifying because His holiness
demands justice. It is misleading to ignore this aspect, and
treat God as a kindly grandfather who will forgive all that has
been thrown in His face by rebellion and total disregard for
His Word, and His provision of grace and mercy. But, He has
provided a Refuge for those who run to it.

## Numbers 36
## Inheritance

The final word in the Book of Wanderings again concerns
inheritance. In Numbers 27:1-4 the fatherless daughters of
Zelophehad received a guarantee that they too would receive
their family's right to an allocation of land. If they married
someone from another tribe, the leaders of their tribe worried,
the land would go to their husbands' tribe, and therefore be lost
to the rightful tribe - in this case the tribe of Manasseh. Moshe
made a ruling that they should marry within the tribe and it
seemed the girls cooperated. Inheritance was also an important
matter to God. Squandering it or treating it with disdain was
frowned upon.

May we treasure the inheritance we have, that of being part
of the family of the God of Israel which was gained for us by
Yeshua, the Jewish Messiah. 1 Peter 1:3-4, "*Blessed be the
God and Father of our Lord Jesus Christ, who according to
His abundant mercy has begotten us again to a living hope
through the resurrection of Jesus Christ from the dead, to an*

*inheritance incorruptible and undefiled and that does not fade away, reserved in heaven for you."*

May we learn to live in a way that honours that inheritance as we continue to glean and live by what is intended for us in the Divine Instructions of the Torah.

The Torah of his God is in his heart; none of his steps shall slide. Psalm 37:31

# DIRECTIONS FROM DEUTERONOMY

The Book of Deuteronomy is one of three books (together with Psalms and Isaiah) most quoted by New Testament authors. It is also one of three books found in the Dead Sea Scroll collection in Qumran that have the greatest number of copies. The anglicized name of this book is from the Greek meaning the 'second law', but its Hebrew name is *Devarim*, which means 'Words'. We will look at the '<u>Words</u> of Moses/*Moshe*' which can be better described as a sermon on the Torah. It is not a 'second' law/*torah*.

The Israelites are about to enter the Promised Land after 39 years and 11 months wandering around in the wilderness. They are finally taking hold of what God has promised. Despite his personal disappointment at not taking them in himself, Moshe, the caring mediator and deliverer, is using these last weeks of his life to remind, exhort, and warn his people to remember what they have learned through the difficulties, failures and victories of their wilderness wandering.

Peter/*Kefar*, our Master's disciple and one of the leaders of the congregation/*kehila* in Jerusalem, could have been echoing Moshe when he said in 2 Peter 1:13-15, "*Yes, I think it is right, as long as I am in this tent (body), to stir you up by reminding you knowing that shortly I must put off my tent, just as our Lord Jesus Christ showed me. Moreover I will be careful to ensure that you always have a reminder of these things after my decease.*"

We will not read in Deuteronomy as we've done previously, that '*the LORD spoke...*' but instead, '*Moshe spoke*'...as in chapter 1, verse 1. He spoke as God's representative. And he was also God's appointed teacher, referred to in Judaism as Moses our Teacher/*Moshe Rabenu*. We will do well to listen along with these one-time slaves, now in covenant with Almighty God, because sometimes we stand on the brink of a new era in our life, stepping into unknown futures.

## Deuteronomy 1
## Remembering

Note in Deuteronomy 1:1-4 the details of location and time. One name mentioned, *Dizahab*, is found nowhere else in the Bible. *Dizahab* is actually from two Hebrew words that literally mean 'enough gold'. The Jewish sages thought it referred to the serious episode of the Golden Calf and it was a sober reminder that the idolatry came about, among other reasons, because of abundant possessions that enabled such an expensive idol to be made. Possessions can easily lead away from dependence on God, therefore - enough gold! Other scholars link it with a place called Dahab, a cape on the western shore of the Gulf of Akaba.

With each reference to a place name, there would be an association with something significant. Perhaps miracles, or successes or even failures would come to mind. The names were reminders that the Israelites had not always trusted God even when surrounded by His miracles and supernatural provision. And once they crossed into Canaan, the Promised Land, the signs and wonders and miraculous provision would not be there in the same measure. New challenges awaited them and they would soon have to provide for themselves by settling the land and all that would entail. Would they trust God under these very different circumstances?

Before they enter the Land though, verses 9-18 record Moshe's recounting of how a justice system was set up within the large congregation in the early days of their journey. We begin to see some things from the perspective of Moshe, some background details that were not always clear in the previous Books. It seems that Moshe had been crying out to the LORD regarding his burden of responsibility and Jethro/*Yitro* was the answer to that problem. His appearance at the right time to give wise advice is recorded in Exodus 18:13-19. After observing his son-in-law sit all day judging disputes and explaining God's laws he warned him that he was in danger of wearing out and advised him to seek helpers.

We have noted in the previous studies that Moshe's leadership is a role model in humility. Here he listened to wise advice and shared the responsibilities by appointing elders to judge minor matters. We also note something else. He says to the people in Deuteronomy 1:9-10, *"And I spoke to you at that time, saying: I alone am not able to bear you. The LORD your God has multiplied you, and here you are today, as the stars of heaven in multitude..."*

Even while telling them the vast number of people had been a burden, he counters that negative connotation with a blessing in verse 11, *"May the LORD God of your fathers make you a thousand times more numerous than you are, and bless you as He has promised you."* Let our words bring encouragement and not condemnation.

In Deuteronomy 1:19-46, Moshe continues to speak of their arrival in Kadesh Barnea where they had been poised to move into the Promised Land. We learn some additional background to what happened there. It seems sending in the spies (scouts) was at the request of the leaders, and therefore Moshe took their request to God, which we know he did each time he was confronted by a dilemma. God instructed him in Numbers 13:1-3 to send in spies, or as explained in *'Wisdom in the Wilderness'* – 'scouts' which is a more accurate translation. We know the disastrous story with its terrible consequences that followed their unbelief and disobedience. We noted from the Numbers passage that their brothers, fellow Israelites, had discouraged the people with a negative report, but here in Deuteronomy 1:28, Moshe confirms that sad situation with the words the people had said to him back then *"...our brethren have discouraged our hearts..."* These words explain the reason for the fear which gripped them. They listened to words of discouragement rather than the words of encouragement concerning God's promises from Joshua and Caleb in Numbers 14:8-9: *"If the LORD delights in us, then He will bring us into this land and give it to us, 'a land which flows with milk and honey'. Only do not rebel against the LORD, nor fear the people of the land, for they are our bread; their protection has departed from them, and the LORD is with us. Do not fear them."*

And Moshe added his own inspiring words at that time. They were not recorded in Numbers, but what he said to the people back then is recorded here in Deuteronomy 1:29-31 and especially, verse 31, *"...God carried you as a man carries his son..."* All these words speak of the sureness of the security we have in God even when facing the unknown. However, the Children of Israel had not listened to those inspiring words either. Later the rebellion was compounded by the people trying to go into Canaan after all, in spite of God saying no. It was too late to regain that which God had previously intended for them. The opportunity was lost! This is a sombre reminder to us all to move in God's timing and purposes for our lives.

## Deuteronomy 2 & 3
## Choosing the right battles

In Deuteronomy 2:1-6, and in many other places later, the people are reminded that God is their guide and instructor. In 2:7 they are also reminded He is their Provider. We know from our previous studies that there were times they doubted all those attributes. And we know it is often only in hindsight as we look back to a 'wilderness' period as Moshe was doing for the Children of Israel, that we realize God was there for us as He was for them, our unseen Guide and Provider. He is the Preparer of the Way too. We read in the words of Deuteronomy 2:30-31 that God had already put fear of the approaching Israelites into the heart of the stubborn King Sihon. The battle that ensued is recorded in Numbers 21:23-26. The victory was theirs because God had decreed it.

In the rest of the second chapter of Deuteronomy and into chapter 3, Moshe recounts the victories in battles they were told to undertake. At other times, they were instructed not to engage in battle. A good principle – let the Holy Spirit choose our battles and not us.

Something else of interest is the many references to giants, both here and in other places in the scriptures. Their existence was one of the reasons for fear among the scouts in Numbers 13:33 NIV, *"We saw the Nephilim there (the descendants of Anak come from the Nephilim). We seemed like grasshoppers in our own eyes, and we looked the same to them."* Perhaps as mentioned before, they were the descendants of the hybrid offspring of the fallen angels of Genesis 6:2 and Jude 6. A fascinating and important subject, but not one we will delve into here. To understand more of the significance of these mysterious beings, particularly relating to our own times, I recommend 'Floodgates', a book written by David Parsons, media spokesperson for ICEJ and available through www.icej.org.

Perhaps they were just a race of large and powerful stature. For now, something we can draw from this emphasis on the might of the giants is that there does not need to be fear of 'giants' in our lives as long God directs our battles. In Amos 2:9 the prophet details how God did just that for the Israelites, *"Yet I destroyed the Amorite before them, whose height was like the height of the cedars, And he was as strong as the oaks..."*

In Exodus 34:24 God had promised to, *"... cast out nations before you and enlarge your borders."* However, two formidable enemies, Sihon, King of the Amorites, and Og who was a descendant of this race of giants Deuteronomy 3:11, and who was the King of Bashan (today's Golan Heights) stood in the way. However, God defeated them, (Numbers 21:24 and 21:35), and therefore weakened the threats that lay ahead - which is why Moshe could say in Deuteronomy 3:21-22, *"...You have seen all that the LORD your God has done to these two kings; so He will do to all the kingdoms through which you must pass. You must not fear them, for the LORD your God Himself fights for you."*

We have the same assurance in 2 Thessalonians 3:3, *"But the LORD is faithful, who will establish and guard you from the evil one."*

Moshe reveals his personal struggle with disappointment in Deuteronomy 3:23-28. Although he pleaded with the LORD, he was not allowed to go into the Promised Land with the people. He was only to view the Land from afar. In Numbers 20:1-13, the people's complaining and Moshe's exasperation combined to cause anger to rise up in this great leader. He had been told to speak to the rock to bring forth water. He was not told to strike it, as previously. But in his anger, he struck it and thus 'spoiled' the picture that God had embedded in this scenario. The Rock represented the Messiah (see *'Wisdom in the Wilderness'*), who was struck once but then, said Yeshua in John 7:37-38, was the source of *"rivers of living water"*.

Also as the Rabbis teach, by saying in front of that huge crowd, "*Must we bring water for you...*" Numbers 20:10, when it was God who would do the miracle as before, he desecrated the Name of God. The opposite of that serious breach of conduct is to sanctify the Name, an important principle in Judaism and an important one in our walk with God.

Moshe learned that there is not always a positive answer to prayer. His example serves as a lesson for all of us as does Paul's in 2 Corinthians 12:8-9a. "*Concerning this thing I pleaded with the LORD three times that it might depart from me, and He said to me 'My grace is sufficient for you for My strength is made perfect in weakness'.*"

Graciously, Moshe endorses Joshua/*Yehoshua* as God's choice as the new leader.

## Deuteronomy 4
## Unique Status, Unique Responsibility.

After Moshe has concluded his review of their history since their deliverance, he reminds them of their tremendous privilege to have had an encounter with God. They are in covenant with Him and have been given His commandments to live by. We can stand with that chosen company and listen with awe to that reminder, and more soberly to the warnings of ignoring His words and directions for our life. In line with the amazement expressed by Moshe in chapter 4:7 about the uniqueness of his nation, the apostle John/*Yonatan* similarly exclaims in 1 John

3:1a, "*Behold, what manner of love the Father has bestowed on us, that we should be called the children of God.*"

In Deuteronomy 4:1, there are three important words. The first will be repeated many times: '<u>hear</u>'/*shmah*! Its meaning is more than merely listening, it is to absorb with understanding and belief. Secondly they were to hear, in order '<u>to do</u>'/*asah*, sometimes inaccurately translated as observe. Thirdly, it would enable them to '<u>possess</u>', which is also an active word. Belief in God is not passive, it is dynamic. "*But do you want to know, O foolish man, that faith without works is dead,*" says James 2:20. Deuteronomy 4:3-4 gives the example from Numbers 25 when the appalling worship of Baal Peor saw many choose a different way which resulted in death. Those who listened and observed, 'holding fast' to the LORD, that is, 'sticking like glue' to Him (the meaning in Hebrew), continued living.

In Deuteronomy 4:5-8, Moshe speaks of the tremendous privilege of being the recipients of God's righteous Torah. "*So then, the law (Torah) is holy, and the commandment is holy, righteous and good,*" agrees Paul in Romans 7:12 NIV.

Something of what this Torah means to those who accept its precepts, is described in Psalm 19:7-9, "*The law of the LORD is perfect, converting the soul; The testimony of the LORD is sure, making wise the simple; The statutes of the LORD are right, rejoicing the heart; The commandment of the LORD is pure, enlightening the eyes; The fear of the LORD is clean, enduring forever; The judgments of the LORD are true and righteous altogether.*"

The whole of Psalm 119, in which every verse of this long psalm mentions the Word of God in one form or another, also gives an idea of the privilege we have of possessing such a treasure.

Later, in Deuteronomy 4:32-38, the privilege, and unique experience of being chosen by God from out of the nations and deliverance from bondage, is clearly spelt out. We know it foreshadows the experience of all who come to know God. To turn from such grace, or walk in disobedience to His commands seems unthinkable.

And in spite of those privileges, in spite of witnessing the awe-inspiring manifestation of God's Presence as in Deuteronomy 4:11-12, and 32-38, Moshe knew that serious warnings were required. In this chapter as well as other passages, he constantly urges them to 'take heed'; so that they will not forget those things they have seen and now know. How easy it is to turn away from the worship of God. How easy to succumb to temptation. The New Testament contains warnings too of being careful not to fall away. Our Master Yeshua said on Matthew 6:13a to pray, *"...and do not lead us into temptation but deliver us from the evil one."* We dare not become complacent but must take care, (Deuteronomy 4:9), that we are indeed still following the way in which we started out.

Take note of Deuteronomy 4:1 and 5. The words translated as 'statutes' and 'judgments' or 'ordinances' will be seen many times in Deuteronomy but 'statutes' always comes first. This word is literally 'engraved decrees' referring to laws that were engraved on stone by an authoritative body. Judaism teaches that 'decrees' may not have a rational explanation, but because

God has given them, they demand obedience without necessarily understanding the reason why. 'Judgments', or 'ordinances' generally pertain to civic laws and are necessary for society to function in a good and just way.

The keeping of them all is meant to be a testimony as stated in 4:6, "*Therefore be careful to observe them; for this is your wisdom and your understanding in the sight of the peoples who will hear all these statutes, and say, 'Surely this great nation is a wise and understanding people'.*" Would that our lives bring this kind of reaction!

Also, in Deuteronomy 4:9 is a tenet held dear in Judaism: "... *And teach them* (that is the commandments) *to your children and your children's children.*" They take this and other passages seriously such as Exodus 13:8, "*And you shall tell your son in that day, saying, 'This is done because of what the LORD did for me when I came up from Egypt'.*"

And in Deuteronomy 6:6-7, "*And these words which I command you today shall be in your heart. You shall teach them diligently to your children...*"

Paul advocates this important principle in Ephesians 6:4, "*And, you fathers, do not provoke your children to wrath: but bring them up in the training and admonition of the Lord.*"

Another temptation is to reduce God to our image or to worship the works of our own hands, or even to worship the creation, rather than the Creator. Beginning with Deuteronomy 4:15 until verse 40, interspersed with the reminders of their amazing and unique deliverance and their covenantal relationship with the God of the universe, are stern warnings not to make images and not to succumb to false worship because there will be serious consequences. *"For the LORD your God is a consuming fire, a jealous God,"* says Moshe in verse 24. The writer of Hebrews repeats these frightening words in Hebrews 12:29.

There are many instances of judgment wrought, or judgment to come, in which fire is the instrument of fearful and swift punishment, and as mentioned in *'Wisdom from the Wilderness'* when we looked at Numbers 21, the manifestations of God's Presence was often by fire. *"I came to send fire on the earth, and how I wish it were already kindled."* said Yeshua in Luke 12:49 in the context of speaking of judgment on unfaithfulness.

Once God judged the earth with water, but fire will be the medium in the last days as 2 Peter 3:5-7 tells us, *"For this they wilfully forget: that by the word of God the heavens were of old, and the earth standing out of water and in the water, by which the world that then existed perished, being flooded with water. But the heavens and the earth which are now preserved by the same word, are reserved for fire until the day of judgment and perdition of ungodly men."*

There are attributes of God upon which we don't usually dwell very much, preferring the love and goodness aspects, but Romans 11:22 says, *"Therefore consider the goodness and severity of God: on those who fell, severity; but toward you, goodness if you continue in His goodness. Otherwise, you also will be cut off."*

We have been studying His standards for His 'set apart' people throughout these Five Books. Moshe is spelling out the dire consequences for the people if they give their worship and loyalty to another in spite of all they have received. This is a principle for us to heed, "...*For everyone to whom much is given, from him much will be required; and to whom much has been committed, of him, they will ask the more."* Said Yeshua in Luke 12:48.

Note though in Deuteronomy chapter 4, that verses 30-31 declare that even when the Israelites fall and consequently are in distress, they only have to turn back to Him in true repentance and He is there. What grace! And what are the consequences of obedience? Verse 40 is one example - "...*that it may go well with you and your children after you..."*

Deuteronomy 4:41 tells us that three of the six Cities of Refuge were set apart on the east side of the Jordan in which they were camped. We looked at the significance of some of these cities in '*Wisdom from the Wilderness*', Numbers 35.

## Deuteronomy 5
## Mountain Top Experiences

Moshe recounts the unique and incredible experience they had at Mt Sinai, here called Horeb. It is also called the Mountain of God in Exodus 3:1 and some other scriptures including 1 Kings 19:8, when the prophet Elijah was fleeing Jezebel, after he was strengthened he travelled forty days and forty nights until he reached, "...*Horeb, the mountain of God.*" This confirms it was still known by that title in Elijah's time.

As Moshe repeats the Ten Commandments, (more literally the Ten Words), there are slight differences from the first recording of them in Exodus. One difference is found in the commandment concerning the Seventh Day. Deuteronomy 5:12, says to "*observe (or keep) the Sabbath day...*" whereas in Exodus 20:8, it is "*remember the Sabbath Day.*" The two candles which the mother of a Jewish household lights each Friday evening, symbolizes these two commandments – 'remember' and 'observe/keep'.

There are other words in Deuteronomy 5:15 not found in the Exodus account which connects keeping the Seventh Day holy to their deliverance from slavery. In Exodus 20:11, it is tied to creation. "*For in six days the LORD made the heavens and the earth, the sea, and all that is in them, and rested the seventh day. Therefore the LORD blessed the Sabbath day and hallowed it.*"

These two aspects are also acknowledged in the Friday night prayers that welcome Shabbat in the Jewish home and synagogue. God is both Creator and Deliverer.

Something to note is Moshe's role as a mediator, as indicated in Deuteronomy 5:5, and 25-27. As explained in '*Wisdom from the Wilderness*', from Numbers 27, there have only been two mediators in biblical history, Yeshua is the other.

## Deuteronomy 6
## Spiritual Connections

The words *"Hear, O Israel: The LORD our God, the LORD is one!"* from 6:4, are known as the *Shema* and recited morning and evening by religiously observant Jews. They are also the words on their lips at the point of death. It is a statement of covenantal relationship, 'our God'; it is an affirmation of belief in the one God; it is a declaration of what should be the response to that unique relationship, (verse 5). Rabbi Riskin notes that: 'The name translated 'LORD'[42] is *Yud-Heh-Vav-Heh* and implies eternity, ultimate redemption and love. *Elohinu*/our God implies 'power and creativity'. In its entirety, the Shema consists of three paragraphs: Deuteronomy 6:4–9, Deuteronomy 11:13–21 and Numbers 15:37–41.

Jewish commentary also recognizes that the Shema is a prophetic statement and refers to Zechariah 14:9, *"And the LORD shall be King over all the earth. In that day it shall be – 'The LORD is one,' And His name one."* There will come a day when the nations who do not acknowledge God as King, will do so.

We've mentioned before the responsibility given to the Jewish nation to pass on the words of God to succeeding generations. Here in Deuteronomy 6:7 and 20-25, they are again told to observe that responsibility. As we learn to recognize the principles that God has embedded in the Torah for all those

---

[42] LORD denotes the four letter Name of God of which the pronunciation is unknown. Jews do not attempt to pronounce and refer to it as HaShem or in prayer, Adonai.

who follow Him, we can see that this is an important one, as it is referred to several times.

We now look at the beautiful instructions in 6:8-9. These words are understood in a spiritual context but are expressed in a literal way by the Jewish tradition of *'laying tefillin'* and attaching *mezuzot* to every doorway.

*Tefillin* is a pair of small black leather boxes which contain Hebrew verses and are attached to leather straps. One box is wrapped around the left arm in a prescribed manner so that the box rests on the upper arm, and the other is around the head so that the box is on the forehead. The verses are from Exodus 13:1–10; 13:11–16; Deuteronomy 6:4–9; 11:13–21.

Sometimes tefillin is translated as *'phylacteries'* in the New Testament, for example in Matthew 23:5, *"...They make their phylacteries broad."* But this word which has been translated from Greek actually means 'amulet', usually thought of as a protective charm, which the tefillin are not.

The Hebrew word tefillin is related to the word *'tefilah'* (prayer) and they are attached during times of prayer. It has beautiful symbolism because the two boxes containing the scriptures are placed on the forehead and the left arm, representing the intellect as well as action and strength. The left arm too, is commonly thought of as the one connected to the heart, the seat of emotions.

The writer of Proverbs probably has this practice in mind when he writes, *"Let not mercy and truth forsake you: bind them about your neck; write them upon the tablet of your heart.*" Proverbs 3:3. And Proverbs 6:20-21, "*My son, keep your father's command, do not forsake the law of your mother. Bind them continually upon your heart; tie around your neck.*" Again, Proverbs 7:2-3 NIV; "*Keep my commands and you will live, guard my teachings as the apple of your eye. Bind them upon your fingers, write them upon the tablet of your heart.*"

The Jewish practice of 'laying tefillin' as it is called, gives us a wonderful visual picture of applying God's words to our emotions, our intellect, and our actions.

A mezuzah is a small, slim, cylindrical shaped container in which is a roll of parchment containing the scriptures of Deuteronomy 6:4–9; 11:13–21; Numbers 15:37-41. A mezuzah is attached to the right hand side of each entrance to the house, as well as all doorways within the house, in literal obedience to Deuteronomy 6:9, "*You shall write them on the doorposts of your house and on your gates.*" The word mezuzah generally means doorpost in scripture.

My Jewish Learning' https://www.myjewishlearning.com/ says:

'A mezuzah serves two functions: Every time you enter or leave, the mezuzah reminds you that you have a covenant with God; second, the mezuzah serves as a symbol to everyone else that this particular dwelling is constituted as a Jewish household, operating by a special set of rules, rituals, and beliefs'.

Deuteronomy 6:10-19 warns that abundance can result in forgetfulness of God's gracious blessings. It can lead to idolatry, putting trust in other surrounding influences and environments.

Two things we can note in these verses. One is another example of a play on words. The Hebrew word in verse 16 for 'test' or 'tempt', is *'nasa'*. Moshe is referring to the incident in Exodus 17:7, *"So he called the name of the place Massah and Meribah, because of the contention of the children of Israel, and because they tempted (nasa) the LORD, saying, "Is the LORD among us or not?"*

The other is verse 18 in which 'going in and possessing' the land was contingent on them doing the right thing by God who was about to bless them in such an amazing way. As we will see in other warnings to come from Moshe, God can <u>dispossess</u> them even if only for a time.

## Deuteronomy 7
### Commitment or Compromise

The warnings in 7:1-11 are very strong. There were to be no compromises. They were to destroy everything that proclaimed false worship. Verses from 25 to the end of the chapter reiterate the warning.

Loving your neighbour as yourself, (Leviticus 19:18); loving the stranger; compassion and mercy; all are attributes that are embedded in the Torah for God's people at all times. However, they were not to mistake tolerance of pagan practices within the Land that belonged to God, as love. James 1:27 says that not only is compassion for the vulnerable essential to a pure religious belief, but so is keeping oneself free from wrongful influences. *"Pure and undefiled religion before God and the Father is this: to visit orphans and widows in their trouble, and to keep oneself unspotted from the world."* Compromise is dangerous. *"Do not love the world or the things in the world."* Says 1 John 2:15a, and 2 Corinthians 6:14 commands, *"Do not be unequally yoked together with unbelievers. For what fellowship has righteousness with lawlessness? And what communion has light with darkness?"*

They were to guard against unholy alliances that bound them with spiritual bonds such as covenants and marriage. Verses 6-7 tell the reason; these kinds of relationships would turn them from following the God of Abraham. All this proved horribly right in Israel's history. They are a set-apart people! Called for His purposes. Not, Deuteronomy 7:7, because they are better than anyone else or more deserving, but simply because a sovereign God chose them, the least of all peoples so that He could demonstrate His faithfulness even through flawed human beings. This is confirmed in 1 Corinthians 1: 27, *"But God has chosen the foolish things of the world to put to shame the wise, and God has chosen the weak things of the world to put to shame the things which are mighty."*

In Deuteronomy 7:6 is a beautiful word translated 'special' or 'guarded treasure'. It is *'segula'*, that is, a treasure that is specifically for the pleasure of its owner. That is what God's people are to Him. It is first mentioned in Exodus 19:5, *"Now therefore, if you will indeed obey My voice and keep My covenant, then you shall be a special treasure/segula to Me above all people; for all the earth is Mine."*

God refers to His people as His 'segula', several times in Scripture and there is a beautiful promise in Malachi 3:17 NIV, *"On the day when I act, says the LORD Almighty, they will be my treasured possession/segula I will spare them, just as a father has compassion and spares his son who serves him."*

Peter writing to Believers in Messiah Yeshua, calls them a 'segula'. 1 Peter 2:9 says, *"But you are a chosen generation, a royal priesthood, a holy nation, His own special/peculiar people [segula], that you may proclaim the praises of Him who called you out of darkness into His marvellous light."*

Deuteronomy 7:12 is the beginning of a Torah Portion with the name '*Eikev*'. The word 'Eikev' is best translated as 'heel'. The opening verse of the portion translated literally from the Hebrew begins, 'Then it will be as a consequence (Eikev)'. That is, the blessings will come on the 'heels' of following the Divine Command; they are the consequence of obedience as we have learned.

As the positive consequences of obedience continue to be spelt out, a word we can note in 7:14 is 'barren male'. The Hebrew word '*akar*', is only used once in the entire Tanakh. This statement comes millennia before it was discovered by science that males can be barren too. Until relatively recent times, it was always thought the female was at fault when children could not be conceived. The Word of God is well ahead of medical and scientific thinking!

On the brink of something new in our journey with God, fear can come into our thinking. However, victory for the Israelites was guaranteed by the LORD. Moshe reminds them in verse

21 that the reason fear need not overcome them, is because of one simple fact. *"...for the LORD your God, the great and awesome God, is among you."*

'Terrible', 'awesome' are words that may be used in English to convey the Hebrew word *norah*, a God to be reckoned with! We do not serve just any god; the One among us is awesome and fearful to our enemies.

### Deuteronomy 8
### Faith put to the Test

It is made clear in Deuteronomy 8:1-5 and later in 8:15-16 that through adversity God tests to see what is in a man's heart. Adversity reveals how strong our faith is and what our reaction will be, and it often takes place in a desert or wilderness. Even though the Israelites complained and failed many times, here they were holding onto a God they could not see - a concept alien to the nations around them. They were humbled, (verse 3), but not defeated, gradually learning that true life came from the words of God. Yeshua quoted from Deuteronomy 8:3, *"... man shall not live by bread alone..."* in his wilderness testing. (Luke 4:4).

Moshe continues to say in Deuteronomy 8:5 that not only testing, but at times chastening, is required. Hebrews 12:5-6 endorses this, *"...My son, do not despise the chastening of the LORD, Nor be discouraged when you are rebuked by Him; For whom the LORD loves He chastens, And scourges every son whom He receives."*

The Word of God, by the way, takes it for granted that a parent's responsibility is to correct wrong behaviour, even though the methods maybe 'painful' as Hebrew 12:11 says. *"Now no chastening seems to be joyful for the present, but painful; nevertheless, afterward it yields the peaceable fruit of righteousness to those who have been trained by it."* These principles are something to be noted by parents who truly love their children! As well as the spiritual message it is conveying.

The Promised Land awaits them and is a 'good land', a land with abundant blessings. Among them, Deuteronomy 8:7-8 mentions seven species of produce: wheat, barley, grapes, figs, pomegranates, olives, and dates. Although honey may be one of the products listed, it is date honey and not bee honey in this case although bee honey is also referred to in other scriptures. Bee honey does not belong in a list of plants, and there are other reasons too for the scholars to reach this conclusion. These Seven Species are commonly featured on household or ornamental items to which any visitor shopping in Israel will attest. There were other species of fruit growing in Israel as well, so why are only these mentioned? These seven share a common denominator. Nogah Hareuveni, 'Nature in our Biblical Heritage', (1980) explains:

'During the fifty days between Passover and the Feast of Weeks (Shavuot/Pentecost), about from mid-April to mid-June, the flowers of the olive, grape, pomegranate, and date open, and the embryonic figs begin to develop. During the same period, the kernels of wheat and barley fill with starch, and so the fate of the crops of each of the seven varieties is determined'.

Each of these seven species is dependent on an uncertain weather pattern as spring moves into summer. The hot dry wind from the south or east, the cold north wind, rain, and sunshine, are all needed at the right times for this delicate interplay of the ripening fruit. The Israelites observed their pagan neighbours praying to their gods for certain weather conditions, which would be a tempting pattern to follow, except for one thing. It was from these seven only that that the first fruits (Hebrew – *bikkurim*) were to be presented to the LORD as directed in Exodus 23:19a and other scriptures, *"The first of the firstfruits of your land you shall bring into the house of the LORD your God."*

Therefore, the Israelites were required to pray to their One God only, who controls all nature, so that these seven would ripen to the quality worthy of presenting as a first fruit offering to Him.

After listing other benefits of the Land they were about to enter, Deuteronomy 8:10 commands, *"When you have eaten and are full, then you shall bless the LORD your God for the good land which He has given you."* It is because of this verse that although a blessing is offered before a meal, Jews thank God after a meal, and it is quite a lengthy and very lovely prayer. Thanking God after a meal is a reminder that once satisfied when things are going well, we could take blessings and favour for granted and so lose the sense of gratitude we should have before our Father.

Because 8:10 says 'bless', this is a good time to note that the word 'bless' appears many times throughout Scripture. Not only does God speak of blessing His people and His people to bless others, but His Word says many times to bless Him. The Psalms are a special example, such as *"Bless the LORD, O my soul, and forget not all his benefits..."* Psalm 103:2.

The Jewish people are careful to do this, and beginning with the words: *'Baruch Ata Adonai,* (Blessed are you LORD)' they 'bless the LORD their God' many times in a day for His specific gifts to them, including before a snack or piece of fruit, a glass of water and even on seeing a wonderful sight and many other instances. It is a lovely tradition which focuses thoughts on the Giver of good things throughout the day.

*"In everything give thanks; for this is the will of God in Christ Jesus for you,"* says 1 Thessalonians 5:18. Sometimes this is taken to mean to give thanks regardless of what is happening to you, but I believe Jewish Paul is writing from his tradition of giving thanks to God for the many blessings he receives each day.

The Hebrew word *'bracha*/blessing is related to the Hebrew word for 'knee'. The knee is used to bow and thereby recognize authority. Blessing God proclaims His reign over our lives.

Recognising God's authority is a good thing because Deuteronomy 8:11-18 warns of self-importance, of taking credit for achievements and forgetting that any abundance and success is from God. Remembering by the way, that God does not give wealth, but He does give the means to obtain it - 8:18. Forgetting to acknowledge Him is to our peril and can lead to false worship and dishonour.

## Deuteronomy 9
## Warning against self-righteousness

As Moshe repeats what will happen when they cross over the Jordan River, he reminds them in 9:4 that it is not their righteousness that earned them the Land and their victories.

We'll pause here to remember that we are also the recipients of undeserved mercy. This undeserved mercy is something we are reminded of in Titus 3:3-7, *"For we ourselves were also once foolish, disobedient, deceived, serving various lusts and pleasures, living in malice and envy, hateful and hating one another. But when the kindness and the love of God our Savior toward man appeared, not by works of righteousness which we have done, but according to His mercy He saved us, through the washing of regeneration and renewing of the Holy Spirit, whom He poured out on us abundantly through Jesus Christ our Savior, that having been justified by His grace we should become heirs according to the hope of eternal life."*

Continuing in Deuteronomy 9:4-6, the people are told that they are going to dispossess the various nations living in God's Land because of the wickedness of those current inhabitants. It is not because of their own righteousness. In Genesis 15:13-16, we read of the 'Covenant of the Halves' that God made with Abraham, *"Then He said to Abram: 'Know certainly that your descendants will be strangers in a land that is not theirs, and will serve them, and they will afflict them four hundred years. And also the nation whom they serve I will judge; afterward they shall come out with great possessions. Now as for you, you shall go to your fathers in peace; you shall be buried at a good* *old age. But in the fourth generation they shall return here, <u>for the iniquity of the Amorites is not yet complete</u>."*

In other words, there comes a time when the wickedness of a nation reaches a point of deserving God's fearful judgment, and that time had come for the nations in God's Land. It was time to give the land to His people. One of the practices which could no longer be tolerated by God was that of the occult. Deuteronomy 18:9-14 spells out what the nations were involved in, and that is why He was driving them out before the people of Israel.

In most of Deuteronomy chapter 9, Moshe recounts the sin of the Golden Calf, as well as other times of rebellion. He reminds them that they too provoked the LORD to the point of His patience running out, (9:14). It was through the sacrificial intercession of Moshe, their mediator - 9:18 and 25-29 - that God forgave them. Also see 10:10. We have already seen that Moshe was the forerunner, the picture of one who sits at the right hand of God, making intercession. Romans 8:34, *"Who is he who condemns? It is Christ who died, and furthermore is also risen, who is even at the right hand of God, who also makes intercession for us."*

## Deuteronomy 10
## A Privileged People

As Moshe continues the saga of the Golden Calf, the broken tablets and his return up the mountain, he says that he made an 'ark' for the new tablets of stone. 'Ark' is translated from *'aron'* meaning a container. This is not the Ark of the Covenant/

*Aron HaKodesh* which would have been made by Betzalel after the incident to which Moshe is referring. That ark was also wood but it had an overlay of gold. (Exodus 25:10-16). There is some debate between the Jewish sages about the two 'arks' and reconciling various scriptures mentioning them, but the Ramban[43] suggests Moshe's ark of wood was merely a temporary vessel to receive the tablets, and when the tabernacle/ *mishkan* was constructed, the tablets were placed in the one made by Betzalel.

One thing we can draw from the concept of the arks holding Words from the very hands of God and a symbol of the unbreakable covenant He had made with His people, is that we are also 'containers' of a treasure. *"For it is the God who commanded light to shine out of darkness, who has shone in our hearts to give the light of the knowledge of the glory of God in the face of Jesus Christ. But we have this treasure in earthen vessels that the excellence of the power may be of God and not of us."* 2 Corinthians 4:6-7.

We are likened to clay vessels, and like the simple wooden box, hold amazing treasure.

We now look at Deuteronomy 10:12-15 where we learn what is expected from His people by the God who made the universe 10:14, and Who, we have learned by now, has shown them mighty power and incredible mercy. After all, the gods of other

---

[43] Moses ben Nahman, commonly known as Nachmanides, and also referred to by the acronym **Ramban**, was a leading medieval Jewish scholar, Sephardic rabbi, philosopher, physician, kabbalist, and biblical commentator. <u>Wikipedia</u>

nations often demanded appeasement that could even involve child sacrifice. But we read simply in these verses: we are to fear Him, walk in His ways, love Him, serve Him heart and soul. There is a similar scripture in Micah 6:8 *"He has shown you, O man, what is good; and what does the LORD require of you but to do justice and to love kindness and to walk humbly with your God."*

To do this, Moshe advises them to 'circumcise their hearts'. As explained in *'The Elegance of Exodus'* the Hebrew word for circumcision means to restrict or restrain and in the case of physical circumcision for the male, it symbolized restricting natural desires within the boundaries of God's standards. Moshe, and Jeremiah later, use the ritual to urge that spiritually, they keep within God's boundaries. Jeremiah 4:4 NIV, *"Circumcise yourselves to the LORD, circumcise your hearts, you people of Judah and inhabitants of Jerusalem, or my wrath will flare up and burn like fire because of the evil you have done."* Paul agrees with the prophets in Romans 2:29, *"...but he is a Jew who is one inwardly; and circumcision is that of the heart..."*

Read again Deuteronomy 10:12-22. Their God is not just powerful, but a God of justice, a Provider to the vulnerable, the weak, and the outsider! This is their role model, their standard. These verses are amazing! They speak of an amazing God. What a privilege they had and what a privilege we all have who know Him.

## Deuteronomy 11
## Be Aware of Deception

In light of what they just heard, in 11:1, Moshe repeats part of the 'shema' from Deuteronomy 6:5 (*"You shall love the LORD your God..."*). And he repeats more in 11:18-21, ending with the resultant blessings that await the obedient.

Verses 10-17 from chapter 11 touch on an important subject for the Middle East. In Egypt an efficient man-made watering system was used and some of the procedures were foot operated to raise water from the Nile and distribute it through channels to the required areas. However, in the Land of Israel, water distribution would not be by human involvement - they would have to rely on the rain promised by God. It would be an exercise in trust and training them to keep their worship for God alone, because 11:16 warns them to take care that they are not deceived. As mentioned before, it would be a temptation to look to the gods of Canaan who supposedly controlled various kinds of weather. It is so easy to be deceived unless we are diligent, and therefore the New Testament writers had quite a few warnings against deception. *"These things I have written to you concerning those who try to deceive you."* says 1 John 2:26.

Looking forward now to Deuteronomy 11:24, we see a principle that God has embedded for us throughout the Torah and particularly in this Book. There are plenty of promises of God bringing about victory in battle, showering blessings, and forgiving shortcomings. But there are many instances of the Israelites being urged to move forward into battle, or into new territory and other situations usually requiring a step of faith. Here in verse 24, every place is promised to them – but, only where their feet have first trod. Life with God is a partnership with Him. It is not sitting back and expecting Him to do everything. Effort is required from His people and sometimes stepping out in faith comes first before we see God act on our behalf.

Deuteronomy 11:26-32 speaks of an event that would be a powerful picture of choice and is elaborated on later in chapter 27.

## Deuteronomy 12
### Doing things God's Way

In this chapter, verses 1-4 and again in 29-31, are warnings about any association or even curiosity about pagan worship. Although directed specifically to the Israelites about the temptation of idolatry, surely the warning remains for God's people throughout the ages. Do not compromise in the name of 'tolerance' or false neighbourliness. There is no room for spiritual alliances with those who do not acknowledge the God of Israel, the Creator. God gave the Children of Israel specific instructions on how and where to worship. In chapter 12:14, they had to be careful to find the right place, the right times and the right way because God was embedding an important principle for His people for all time.

We will add Deuteronomy 23:17 where God warned not to mix the ways of ungodly religion with worship of the God of Israel.

We need to be careful that our worship and service to the LORD is holy and God honouring.

Note an important word in 12:7 - the word 'rejoice'. Rejoicing was definitely part of worship of the LORD and is included many times in instructions involving worship.

Although sacrifices were still to be offered in the right place, Deuteronomy 12:26 and the warning against partaking of blood to be heeded 12:23, once in Canaan the rules about killing for meat for the household were able to be adapted. In the wilderness journey if they killed for meat, they had to bring it to the door of the tabernacle as we learnt before. Leviticus 17:5 NLT gives the reason: "*The purpose of this rule is to stop the Israelites from sacrificing animals in the open fields. It will ensure that they bring their sacrifices to the priest at the entrance of the Tabernacle, so he can present them to the LORD as peace offerings.*"

The words which begin verse 12:23, 'be sure', are translated from a Hebrew word '*chazak*', a very strong word, meaning they **really** had to be sure. As written in '*Lessons From Leviticus*', the fact that blood is essential to life is indisputable, and its role in atonement renders it sacred.

## Deuteronomy 13
## Corrupting Influences

The warning about avoiding idolatry is continued by saying that even if one of their own people, someone claiming to have prophetic gifts, chapter13:1-5, or even someone from their own family, 13:6, tries to entice them to turn away from what they know is right, they are not to follow but rid themselves of the corrupting influences. It is that serious. The KJV gives a more accurate translation of 13:4, *"Ye shall walk after the LORD your God, and fear him, and keep his commandments, and obey his voice, and ye shall serve him, and cleave unto him."*

The only other time we are told 'to cleave', is Genesis 2:24 KJV, *"Therefore a man should leave his father and mother and cleave unto his wife and they shall be one flesh."* Beware even of signs and wonders, Deuteronomy 13:1-2. Not every miracle is from God.

We have read of so-called 'prophets' in modern times, leading people into false and sometimes bizarre worship with tragic results. It may be that the person did have prophetic gifts, but came into deception themselves. We are each responsible to God and must use discernment, testing new things against God's Word. And enticement can be a test for us to prove our loyalty and commitment, Deuteronomy 13:3. The New Testament writers too warned about deception. It would be good to stop and read the whole of Jude, for example. The Book of Jude has a clear warning about ungodly people and the consequences of their influence.

Also 2 Peter 2:1 is instructive, *"But there were also false prophets among the people, even as there will be false teachers among you, who will secretly bring in destructive heresies, even denying the Lord who bought them, and bring on themselves swift destruction."*

And don't forget Yeshua's warning in Matthew 7:15, *"Beware of false prophets, who come to you in sheep's clothing, but inwardly they are ravenous wolves."*

A very strong principle throughout the Torah, and especially made clear in Deuteronomy, is spelled out here in 13:6, *"...and you must purge the evil from among you."*

I also suggest reading Ezekiel chapter 9 to further understand the seriousness with which God views His people dabbling with, or embracing, that which leads away from the worship of the one true God, or tolerating it in any form.

## Deuteronomy 14
## Outworking of an Inward Holy Life

The opening verses of 14 command the Israelites not to adopt the pagan practices of bodily mutilation to express grief. This is similar to the instruction in Leviticus 19:28 not to make cuttings in their flesh for the dead.

Although grief is accepted as normal, death is not final and therefore should not be terrifying, as it may be for the pagans around them. The new Believers in Messiah learned that lesson from Paul where he says in 1 Thessalonians 4:13 NIV, *"Brothers and sisters, we do not want you to be uninformed about those who sleep in death, so that you do not grieve like the rest of mankind, who have no hope."*

The laws of kashrut[44] are repeated in Deuteronomy 14:3-21 and have been discussed in '*Lessons from Leviticus*'. However, it is good to repeat that the forbidden animals were generally those who fed on carcasses of other animals – dead things. Partaking of things tainted with death and decay does not bring a healthy spiritual life. The psalmist prays in Psalm 119:37 NIV, "*Turn my eyes away from worthless things...*" And Philippians gives some good advice in chapter 4, verse 8 on which to meditate, whatever is noble, just, pure, lovely, and of good report.

The people of Israel were instructed to tithe all their crops and livestock, see Deuteronomy 14:22 to the end of the chapter. They were to give their tithes to the Levites who had no land of their own, but served in the Temple as detailed in Numbers 18:21, "*Behold, I have given the children of Levi all the tithes in Israel as an inheritance in return for the work which they perform, the work of the tabernacle of meeting.*"

The Levites in turn, were to take an offering from the tithes they received and give them to the priests. Along with the First Fruits to be offered to God, tithing laws were an important principle. That is, that which belongs to God is His.

The topic of whether non-Jewish Believers are obligated to tithe will not be addressed in this Study except to say that the principle of setting aside for the work of the Kingdom of God is firmly embedded in Scripture, just like the tithes of Israel supported the work and maintenance of the temple.

---

[44] Dietary laws

Note in Deuteronomy14:26, the commandment to the Levites about exchanging their tithe for silver was not just a dry ritual. It was accompanied by rejoicing. Again the instruction to rejoice! Worship was to be a joyous event and to include the family. Joy is a hallmark of many Jewish traditions. Another aspect to worship is in 14:29. Strangers, widows and orphans, in other words, the lonely and the vulnerable, are not to be ignored in our religious pursuits.

## Deuteronomy 15
## Loving Your Neighbour

The care of the poor and disadvantaged continues to be addressed in this chapter as the structure for a just and ethical society unfolds.

In 15:1-6 we again come across the Seventh Year known as the *shmita*. Leviticus 25:3-4 says there was to be six years of sowing and harvesting but the seventh year was to be a rest year for the fields, a Sabbath year. The farmer had to trust God for provision.

We see another instruction concerning the shmita in Deuteronomy 15:1-6. At the end of every seventh year, all debts of fellow Jews had to be pardoned. Verses 7-11 go on to enlarge the concept of care for those within their community. This is a very important principle and one that was taught to the new Gentile Believers in Yeshua. The 8th and 9th chapters of 2nd Corinthians, for example, teach about caring for poorer members of the Believing Community.

Deuteronomy 15:9 continues the warning against ignoring the plight of the poor. It includes a Hebraic idiomatic expression for an ungenerous spirit. Having an 'evil eye' is to be ungenerous while having a 'good eye' is to be generous.

In Matthew 6:19-24, Yeshua is teaching about not laying up treasure for oneself and uses this expression to denote stinginess, *"...For where your treasure is, there your heart will be also. The lamp of the body is the eye. If therefore <u>your eye is good</u>, your whole body will be full of light. But if <u>your eye is bad</u>, your whole body will be full of darkness. If therefore the light that is in you is darkness, how great is that darkness! No one can serve two masters; for either he will hate the one and love the other, or else he will be loyal to the one and despise the other. You cannot serve God and mammon (wealth)."*

The passage in Deuteronomy 15:16-18 seems to speak of loyalty and love. However we saw in *'The Elegance of Exodus'*, chapter 21, Jewish teaching considers this differently. The fact that a servant would forgo the opportunity for freedom and bind himself to a life of servitude is not looked on kindly within Judaism. Freedom is valued above all.

It is important to note that should your text be translated as 'slave', servant is the better word. As written in *'The Elegance of Exodus'*, chapter 21, the system within the society of Israel bore no resemblance to slavery in which one human being was owned and controlled by another. It was an opportunity to pay off debts or simply just to earn some money.

There are some differences in the instructions about the release of debts and bonded servants from a similar passage in Leviticus, but our current Study does not go into the depth and details of every aspect of the Torah, although they are fascinating and revealing. We are looking for the principles, patterns, and pictures that God has embedded into these Books, including the Mosaic Law, from which we as Christian Believers can mould our lives to also serve a holy God. What we can learn from this and other passages that deal with the bonded servant system, is that compassion for those less fortunate than ourselves, while affording them dignity, is woven into the laws that were to govern the people of God.

## Deuteronomy 16
## Appointments with God

This chapter details observance of what is sometimes referred to as the three 'Pilgrim' Festivals. In Hebrew, they are called *Shalosh HaRegalim,* literally the 'Three of the Feet'. This is because the males at least, were commanded to appear before God in Jerusalem three times a year, 16:16. The way of travel to these feasts was of course, by foot.

Verses 1-8 are about the Day of Pesach and the following seven days, the Feast of Unleavened Bread/*Hag Hamatzot.* Verses 9-12 are concerning the Feast of Weeks/*Shavuot* (also known by Christians as Pentecost). Verses 13-15 are of the Feast of Tabernacles or Booths/*Succot.*

We have previously looked at the Feasts in '*Wisdom from the Wilderness'* and '*Lessons from Leviticus'*. Now they are dealt with here in Deuteronomy for the third time because they are so important. They are also referred to as 'Appointments with the LORD'. God gave former slaves who had no control over how they spent their time, the gift of being in control of time. And the *hagim*, the cyclic yearly feasts, were opportunities to put aside their time for the LORD. They were to pause and remember His goodness, His miracles, His provision and to be reminded of their unique relationship with Him.

And they also provide an important picture for His non-Jewish people, that is, to control time and not let it control us; to pause and remember what God has done in our lives; to remember that there are seasons to life. They also provide a prophetic picture as we remind ourselves that Yeshua was crucified on the day the lambs were killed for the Pesach meal. He rose on the day the First Fruits (a sheaf of barley) were presented. The seven day Feast of Unleavened Bread/*Hag Hamatzot* speaks of the perfect unblemished Bread of Life broken for us. Feast of Weeks/*Shavuot*, (or Pentecost) the first ingathering of the harvest, is a picture of the beginning of the harvest of Believers in Yeshua and, after a long gap, the Feast of Tabernacles/*Succot,* speaks of the final ingathering, still to come. Other special days not mentioned in the Deuteronomy account, Feast of Trumpets/ *Yom HaTeruah* and Day of Atonement/*Yom Kippur,* will be fulfilled in Messiah's coming and reign.

### The Seriousness of Justice

Deuteronomy 16:18 is the beginning of a Portion of the Week/ *Parashat Hashavua,* called *Shoftim,* 'Judges'. Moshe instructs the people of Israel to appoint judges and law enforcement officers in every city. A well-known saying - 'justice, justice you shall pursue' - is taken from 16:20. The Hebrew word for justice is '*tzedak*' which can also be translated as 'righteousness'. Saying something double in the Hebrew Scriptures signifies something very important, a double emphasis. Righteous justice is therefore emphasised here. Such justice includes unbiased and meticulous judgement which is spelt out in Deuteronomy 16:18-17:13 and 19:14-21. The perversion of justice was included in the curses which would later be declared in Deuteronomy 27:19.

Administering justice is to be without corruption or favouritism; crimes must be meticulously investigated and evidence thoroughly examined; a minimum of two credible witnesses is required for conviction and punishment. The strong emphasis and warnings about justice are part of the humane legislation of the Torah, and is a condition of coming into all that God has for His people, see 16:20.

We saw earlier in '*Lessons from Leviticus*' in Leviticus 19 that among all the instructions for holy living, exercising justice was an important component, and that chapter pointed out what justice means for a holy people. Justice includes ensuring the poor of society are cared for, as in Psalm 82:3, *"Defend the poor and fatherless; Do justice to the afflicted and needy."* Honest dealings in business and other interactions are expected, and later emphasised by Ezekiel 45:10 NLT, *"Use only honest weights and scales and honest measures, both dry and liquid."*

Exercising fairness in the courts of justice was reinstated by the righteous king Jehoshaphat following a long period of neglect by a backslidden nation, as recorded in 2 Chronicles 19:4-11 when he brought the people back to the LORD and appointed judges in the cities of Judah. He said to the judges, in verses 6-7, "*...Take heed to what you are doing, for you do not judge for man but for the LORD, who is with you in the judgment. Now therefore, let the fear of the LORD be upon you; take care and do it, for there is no iniquity with the LORD our God, no partiality, nor taking of bribes.*"

Justice is a theme that is repeated many times in the Torah and rolls on through the psalms and prophets. It covers all aspects of life. "*Righteousness and justice are the foundation of Your throne; Mercy and truth go before Your face.*" says Psalm 89:14. God rules with righteousness and justice and that is what He expects from His people. "*...And what does the LORD require of you?*" asks Micah in 6:8, he continues, "*But to do justly, to love mercy, and to walk humbly with your God.*" Here justice and mercy are teamed together.

The New Testament continues the principle of justice in all our dealings. Note James 2:1-4, "*My brethren, do not hold the faith of our Lord Jesus Christ, the Lord of glory, with partiality. For if there should come into your assembly a man with gold rings, in fine apparel, and there should also come in a poor man in filthy clothes, and you pay attention to the one wearing the fine clothes and say to him, 'You sit here in a good place', and say to the poor man, 'You stand there,' or, 'Sit here at my footstool', have you not shown partiality among yourselves, and become judges with evil thoughts.*"

## Deuteronomy 17
## Right Leadership

It is interesting that a severe warning of false worship follows the theme of justice in chapter 16:21 through to chapter 17:5. It can lead to idolatry, leading to a death sentence in order to purge the evil. From verses 6-16 of the same chapter, again the correct administration of justice, especially to do with capital punishment, is spelt out.

God is a God of justice and order and this principle is necessary for both a functioning society and the family of God. Many fail-safe justice principles follow later as in Deuteronomy 19:15-21 which deals with the testimony of witness and 24:17 which warns against the perversion of justice when the more vulnerable are involved. The prophets railed against injustice, particularly when it disadvantaged widows and orphans.

Deuteronomy 17:9-13, expands the principle of justice by acknowledging times when guidance is needed from spiritual leaders. And, in verses 12 and 13, a dire warning for those who do not abide by the correction that comes from them. We should not be rebellious - failing to heed correction and leadership can lead to spiritual death. Part of a pastor's duties, Paul told Timothy, was to *"Preach the word! Be ready in season and out of season. Convince, **rebuke**, exhort, with all longsuffering and teaching."* 2 Timothy 4:2.

Deuteronomy 17:14-20, is the only place in the Torah that speaks of a potential king of Israel. Moshe knew through the inspiration of God's Spirit, that the time would come when the nation would demand a king over them. That time happened in 1 Samuel 8:4-5. Did God intend them to have a king or not? In 1 Samuel 8:7 He told the prophet that by requesting a king they were rejecting Him but to acquiesce to their demand anyway. However, I believe that although Israel was rejecting the sole kingship of the LORD and wanting to be like other nations, knowing their hearts, He did intend them to experience an earthly king. In this passage in Deuteronomy, God gives the guidelines for the kind of king that His nation should have. One of His choosing; one from their own people; one that does not amass wealth or military might. The injunction not to have multiple wives was a reference to the diplomatic alliances made by marriages. It would mean that by doing so the king would be making strong connections with pagan nations. He was also to write down the Words of God, read and heed them. All this was to prevent him, Deuteronomy 18-20, from becoming arrogant, putting himself above his people.

Psalm 72:12-13 gives details of what was, in fact, the role of a Jewish king. Among them was concern for the welfare of his people: *"For he will deliver the needy when he cries, the poor also and him who has no helper. He will spare the poor and needy and save the souls of the needy."* This idyllic psalm is ascribed to King Solomon, and this particular king certainly started his life as a king by asking for nothing more than wisdom in order to rule his people in the way God wanted - 2 Chronicles 1:10, *"Now give me wisdom and knowledge, that I may go out and come in before this people; for who can judge this great people of Yours?"*

Sadly, as we well know, Solomon and most of the kings who followed him did all the things Moshe said they were not to do. God wanted His people to know that an earthly king is not always a good idea, but having a king is within His will. One day he would supply 'The King', the One to whom Psalm 72 alludes. The Jewish sages agree that this is a psalm with Messianic connotations and is speaking of the day when King Messiah will reign. Psalm 72 speaks of a king who serves as well as a king who reigns.

## A Servant King

Isaiah 42 is a chapter which speak of God's servant. These verses are speaking of Israel as his appointed servant but it is obvious that the servant role is not limited to Israel, because some of the achievements prophesied are beyond the scope of an earthly, flawed people. Chapter 42 tells of a gentle servant but one who will bring justice to the whole earth. Only a servant who has both power and authority can do this. Matthew 12:18 quotes Isaiah 42:1-4 in relationship to Yeshua and his future role, "*Behold! My Servant whom I have chosen, My Beloved in whom My soul is well pleased! I will put My Spirit upon Him, And He will declare justice to the Gentiles.*" This proclamation followed a time of many miracles, a time of popularity when the crowds wanted to make him king by force because they were indeed looking for the king they knew would one day be sent to them. "*Therefore when Jesus perceived that they were about to come and take Him by force to make Him king, He departed again to the mountain by Himself alone.*" John 6:15.

God says through Moshe in Deuteronomy 17:15a, *"you shall surely set a king over you whom the LORD your God chooses..."* He additionally says in Psalm 2:6, *"Yet I have set My king on My holy hill of Zion."* One day a righteous King will reign not only over Zion but over the whole world.

## Deuteronomy 18
## The Leader and his People

We have already read about the laws concerning the Levites, particularly in the Book of Numbers, (see *'Wisdom from the Wilderness'*) their assigned roles and the responsibilities of the community to them. As some of those rulings are repeated here in chapter 18:1-8 let us be reminded of a principle alluded to by Paul in 1 Corinthians 9:13 NLT, when he was giving up his rights of being provided for by the congregations, *"Don't you realize that those who work in the temple get their meals from the offerings brought to the temple? And those who serve at the altar get a share of the sacrificial offerings."*

It is also spelt out in 1 Timothy 5:17-18 NIV, *"The elders who direct the affairs of the church well are worthy of double honor, especially those whose work is preaching and teaching. For Scripture says, 'Do not muzzle an ox while it is treading out the grain', and 'The worker deserves his wages'."* Those who labour in the Kingdom of God, giving up their opportunities of a regular income, should be supported by those who have the means.

Another important Torah principle is found in 18:9-14. It is that they were not to have anything to do with any form of spiritual guidance apart from God. This is what the nations did who turned away from God, and remember that after the flood there would have been knowledge of the One God. But seeking guidance from sources other than Him can result in occultist practices. This was a reason nations were to be expelled from the land that belonged to God and which He was going to give to His set-apart people. Jeremiah 10:2 confirms, *"Thus says the LORD: 'Do not learn the way of the Gentiles; Do not be dismayed at the signs of heaven, For the Gentiles are dismayed at them'."*

In Deuteronomy 18:13 they were told they were to be blameless/ *tamim* before the LORD. The word, *'tamim'* describes what the sacrifices brought before the LORD should be, that is without blemish. Seeking out other guides is not following God wholeheartedly or trusting Him with our future. David says in Psalm 26:1 NIV, *"Vindicate me, LORD, for I have led a blameless/ be'tumi, (*a derivative of tamim) *life; I have trusted in the LORD and have not faltered."*

We should aim to have David's simple trusting faith in God alone. If we do, we are not deceived by voices that are not from God, as warned about in Deuteronomy 18:17-22, because one day God said, He will raise up a Prophet like Moshe, who was a Deliverer, a Leader, a Servant. May Israel and the nations of the world, recognize this voice. It is worthwhile here to include an article from *Hebrew4christians*: https://www.hebrew4christians.com/

'Like the patriarch Joseph before him, Moshe was a 'picture' of Yeshua in various significant ways. Though he was a Jew from the tribe of Levi, he appeared as a 'Prince of Egypt' to his own people and was educated in all the wisdom of the Egyptians (Acts 7:22). And though he was God's chosen deliverer, Moses was initially rejected by the Israelites and then turned to the Gentiles, taking a 'foreign bride'. After being severely tested in the desert, he was empowered by God's Spirit to become Israel's deliverer for their hour of great tribulation. Indeed, both Moses and Yeshua were "sent from a mountain of God" to free Israel. Both revealed the meaning of God's Name; both spoke with God "face to face." Moses was sent from (physical) Mount Sinai in Midian; Yeshua was sent from a spiritual "Mount Zion" in Heaven (Heb. 12:22)'.

# Deuteronomy 19
# The Contamination of Guilt

The Cities of Refuge are first alluded to in Exodus 21:12-13 where God provides instructions about an accidental killing and says He will appoint a place for the offender to flee.

In '*Wisdom from the Wilderness*', Numbers 35, the instructions regarding these cities were spelt out and we looked at some of the beautiful pictures in this provision. The Cities of Refuge demonstrate the grace of God and in Deuteronomy 19:8-9, if there is more territory, there is more grace. Joshua 20:7-9 is the account of the Israelites setting up those cities.

The Cities of Refuge were also a part of the justice system that God gave Israel. Someone who caused an accidental death was to be protected, so innocent blood would not be shed by an

Avenger. At the same time, the deliberate shedding of innocent blood called for punishment so that the guilt of that murder is removed from the land. (Deuteronomy 19:11-13).

Before we leave this subject, let's be reminded of what our Master said in Matthew 5:21-22a, "*You have heard that it was said to those of old, 'You shall not murder, and whoever murders will be in danger of the judgment'. But I say unto you that whoever is angry with his brother without a cause shall be in danger of the judgment.*" God views the taking of a life, a life made in His image, extremely seriously. Yeshua is using that commandment to teach that blind anger is also serious. Feelings of hatred may not result in murder, but the underlying root is the same.

The justice system continues to be spelt out from Deuteronomy 19:15 to the end of the chapter with the standard that accusations must be made by more than one witness, and there are serious consequences for a false witness. Note again that the famous 'eye for an eye' verse is an idiom only. Not only is mutilation of the body not permitted in Judaism, but it was to do with appropriate compensation for injury. We looked at the explanation in '*Lessons from Leviticus*' chapter 24.

Verse 14 of Deuteronomy 19, is part of the justice principles that were to be a hallmark of a society that was guided by a just God. Moving your neighbour's boundary marker was serious enough to be part of the list of curses later in Deuteronomy 27:17. Moving a boundary marker was a serious crime in ancient Middle Eastern culture and amounted to theft of property. However, I think this is also something of which the Church has been guilty relating to Judaism. The Church removed the 'landmarks', the boundaries that defined their lifestyle of following the God who chose them and gave them those boundaries. It did it by disparaging and dismissing the Torah, and the Covenants. Even though in our eyes, in today's Judaism the various laws may have been stretched to include many more rules and regulations, dismissing the Mosaic Law as out dated and irrelevant is arrogance. This disdain of the Torah has contributed to the opinion of the Jews that Yeshua cannot possibly be their Messiah. The Church's history towards the Jews is shameful. It includes persecution and many other criminal acts, as well as the burning of Jewish writings.

## Deuteronomy 20
## Fit for battle

Facing an enemy is a fearful thing especially a formidable one as described in verse 1. The Israelites did not have weapons of iron let alone chariots. But words with which we should be very familiar, should ring in our ears. *"Fear not! Don't be afraid!"* The armies of both ancient and modern Israel have had to face overwhelming odds, and apart from the battles in which they've gone against the clear direction of God, they have experienced amazing victories.

We can apply the principle of 'God on our side' in another kind of battle which we face. A battle which the sages of Israel recognized and is recorded in the Talmud: 'Your evil inclination gets up every morning to kill you'. The New Testament writers concur. Romans 7:23, *"But I see another law in my members warring against the law of my mind and bringing me into captivity to the law of sin which is in my members.*" In the same way, as Moshe's recalling of the miraculous deliverance from Egypt in Deuteronomy 20:1, remembering God's miracles in past times in our lives can and should encourage us as we face our own battles.

## Affording Dignity to the Weaker Member

In 20:5-7, various reasons are provided for men to be excused from service in the army. Excusing these men meant, not only was there a force of more focused soldiers, but in verse 8, it bestowed dignity even on those who were fearful. They could leave along with others, without their weakness being seen by all.

Allowing a person dignity is preserved in other commandments, such as Deuteronomy 24:10-11 when going to claim a debt from someone. The lender had to stay outside his house in order to avoid humiliating him in front of his family. Also, the rules at harvest-time we have come across before, and are again given in Deuteronomy 24:19-22, afford dignity to the poor person with the opportunity to gather food for the family without asking for handouts.

We should take notice of this principle. We need to give the same dignity to all, especially the poor. After hearing of a disgraceful gathering in the church at Corinth, Paul asks in 1 Corinthians 11:22, "*What! Do you not have houses to eat and drink in? Or do you despise the church of God and shame those who have nothing? What shall I say to you? Shall I praise you in this? I do not praise you."* And in other places the Tanakh and the New Testament give instructions about honouring the poor.

## Holy War

In approaching a hostile city, the Israelites were first to offer peace as in 20:10. However, should that be refused according to the terms stated, annihilation had to be carried out. Why this harsh decree? Verse 18 provides an answer: by allowing them to remain meant there would be a danger of being influenced by their abominable practices. Leviticus 18:6-28 tells the Israelites that sexual immorality, including incest, in Canaan had reached a point where the land was defiled and waiting to 'vomit' them out. Idolatry was another reason that specific nations were cast out. Idolatry included child sacrifice and could influence and turn away the people of God from their mission of bringing the light of Torah to the world. I Kings 21:25-26, *"But there was no one like Ahab who sold himself to do wickedness in the sight of the LORD because Jezebel his wife stirred him up. And he behaved very abominably in <u>following idols, according to all that the Amorites had done, whom the LORD had cast out</u> before the children of Israel."*

In Genesis 15:13 and 16 the LORD tells Avraham regarding the affliction of his descendants, *"But in the fourth generation they shall return here, for the iniquity of the Amorites is not yet complete."* The sin of the inhabitants of Canaan had to reach depths so bad, that God could not tolerate them in the Land that He had chosen for His people. We can be sure that their depravity was extremely bad. Of course, we know that sadly not all these extremely sinful nations were dealt with by the Israelites in the way God commanded, and idolatrous influences did cause Israel to fall many times, bringing God's judgment on them.

In 1 Corinthians 5, in light of serious sexual sin being tolerated amongst the believing community, Paul used the Feast of Unleavened Bread as a picture to show that even a little sin can influence a whole group. "*Your boasting is not good. Don't you know that a little yeast leavens the whole batch of dough? Get rid of the old yeast, so that you may be a new unleavened batch—as you really are. For Christ, our Passover lamb, has been sacrificed.*" 1 Corinthians 5:6-7 NIV.

The slaughter God authorizes in passages as in Deuteronomy 20:10-18 may cause our modern Western minds discomfort, no matter what God's reasons. Many prefer to think only of a God of love, ignoring His holiness and His justice. But we cannot mould God into our image. Should we feel more comfortable with the New Testament, then we should read Revelation, to see that God, through His Messiah, will one day bring a terrifying judgment on a world which has turned its back on their Creator. Revelation 6:16-17 says, "*and said to the mountains and the rocks, 'Fall on us and hide us from the face of Him who sits in the throne and from the wrath of the Lamb. For the great day of His wrath has come and who is able to stand'?*"

The paradigms of war continue to be drawn in Deuteronomy 20:19. Fruit trees were not to be cut down. There may be a need for wood for a ramp during a siege or for other wooden structures or for fuel, but fruit trees were off-limits. We know that wars can deprive communities of food, and tragically modern war-fare has resulted in land denuded of foliage. But here is a humane law and an environmental one too.

## Deuteronomy 21
## The Righteousness of Society and Family

Chapter 21:1-9 seems to be an insertion which may not be a law dealing with warfare that some scholars claim. There are many factors that can produce an environment in which murder comes easily, and during wartime, the value of life can be devalued and an unexplained death shrugged off. However, the violent death of someone anytime is the responsibility of a community. God told Cain in Genesis 4:10, "*the voice of your brother's blood cries out to Me from the ground.*"

In a way we may find hard to comprehend, murder defiles the land itself and from it, the shed blood cries for justice. Numbers 35:33 told us that blood, that is the taking of life, pollutes the land and demands the life of the murderer to atone for it.

To seek atonement from the LORD for the defilement of an unexplained violent death, a ritual had to be followed. Deuteronomy 21:4 details of how 'running', that is 'living' water, carries away the defilement represented by the heifer's blood flowing in the stream. A heifer has not borne offspring and so it is representative of the person murdered. Not only has that life ended, but so has the lives of his or her unborn descendants. We have seen before that from the beginning, God makes clear that human life is to be valued.

Note that the elders of the community washed their hands (verse 6) in a symbolic act to dispel the community's guilt. This was a Jewish tradition but was not common in Greek or Roman culture. Therefore, it is interesting that Pontius Pilate washed his hands as a way of distancing himself from the sentence he passed on Yeshua. Matthew. 27:24, *"When Pilate saw that he could not prevail at all, but rather that a tumult was rising, he took water and washed his hands before the multitude, saying, "I am innocent of the blood of this just Person. You see to it."* Perhaps this was actually a mocking gesture, using a Jewish tradition to pass the guilt onto the Jews.

Deuteronomy 21:10-14 introduces further rules in times of battle, bringing moral restraints during a time when many normal restraints could be thrown off. Unlike other cultures, a captured young woman, desired by a soldier had to be offered marriage rights and therefore status; she was not merely a spoil of war. First, she was allowed a time of grieving which was also a cooling-off period for the man, (perhaps the shaved head lessened the physical attraction?) and perhaps saved a great deal of unhappiness from wrong and rushed decisions. Note too that changing her clothes and altering her appearance was the first step in changing her culture. If she was to become one of God's family, her old life and ways had to go. A wonderful picture to be heeded.

From laws of warfare to family matters. Chapter 21:15-17 addresses the rights of the First Born. The firstborn of a family had a special status. Until the tribe of Levi was set aside to be the priesthood, the firstborn undertook priestly duties on behalf of his family. He also received a double portion of inheritance and assumed leadership of the family or clan. The importance of firstborn status therefore, is a picture for us from a time and culture far removed. Our Messiah is called God's Firstborn and therefore verses like Colossians 1:18 have more significance when we understand the background. *"He is the beginning, the firstborn from the dead, that in everything he might be pre-eminent."*

Continuing with family concerns, Deuteronomy 21:18-21 again speaks about getting rid of evil in their midst and is a theme which surfaces many times. Unlike some of the ancient cultures, Israelite parents did not have the power of life and death over their children. When all correction failed for a stubborn and rebellious son, the community had the final say. Note that the words 'stubborn' and 'rebellious' are extremely strong in Hebrew. The situation also meant that the 5th commandment, to honour your parents, had been broken. It was the community, not the parents who made the decision. Apparently though, the Rabbis say this has never been carried out. However, in light of this ruling, the parable of the 'Prodigal Son' would have made a huge impact on the listeners. Again, although it seems a harsh ruling in our ears, 21:21b is the principle that is firmly and regularly embedded within the Torah, *"so you shall put away the evil from among you."*

Finally in 21:22-23, we recognize two things in relation to Yeshua's crucifixion. He not only became sin but was also cursed by God, *"...Messiah having become a curse for us..."*

Galatians 3:13 goes on to cite the Deuteronomy verse, "*Cursed is everyone who is hanged on a tree...*" A criminal deserving death was 'hung' on a tree or stake as an example. (At what price our redemption!) We also see why there was a hurry to bury Yeshua. This injunction, "*...his body shall not remain all night on the tree...*" was obeyed by Joshua when he captured Ai. "*And he hanged the king of Ai on a tree until evening. And at sunset Joshua commanded, and they took his body down from the tree...*" Joshua 8:29. Also see Joshua 10:26. In Yeshua's case as well, it was near the beginning of the first day of Passover which made it doubly urgent to take a Jewish body down from a Roman cross.

## Deuteronomy 22
## Developing a Caring Community

A responsibility to care is a theme throughout the Torah and is a principle that should be part of the DNA of all God's people. Note that care for animals is included as in Deuteronomy 22:4 where helping a tired or overloaded animal is part of the 'caring package'. In Exodus 23:4-5, there is the same commandment concerning lost or distressed animals spoken of here in Deuteronomy 22:1-4, but in the Exodus passage the injunction was to include those of 'an enemy'. Another place of care for animals is found later in Deuteronomy 25:4 and is quoted by Paul in 1 Corinthians 9:9-11, speaking of the right of spiritual leaders to benefit materially by those they work among. "*For it is written in the law of Moses,' You shall not muzzle an ox while it treads out the grain...*"

Deuteronomy 22:8 extends the responsibility of care to the wider community.

There are many injunctions to the new Believers in the New Testament in relation to being caring including 1 Thessalonians 5:15, *"...do good to one another and to <u>everyone</u>."*

In regard to concern for animals, it is extended to birds in Deuteronomy 22:6-7 which, although they were not the same value as a domestic beast of burden, were nevertheless, God's creatures. Although it was probably rare that birds' eggs or young chicks would be suitable for food, by 'sending the mother away' as the Hebrew word, *'shalach'* makes clear, her instincts as a mother are protected and honoured. She is relieved of the pain of seeing her young being taken. The same consideration for the mother-young bond is shown in Leviticus 22:27-28.

Interestingly, Deuteronomy 22:7 says that the reward for obeying this rule is a long life. The only other time 'long life' is promised as a reward for obedience of a commandment is 'honouring your mother and father'. One interpretation suggests that the connection is that just as parents sacrifice themselves for the child, so the mother bird, who normally would never linger near a person, will stay and protect her young, thereby risking her own life. It is honouring the God-given parent/child relationship, found throughout nature.

## Pure Relationships

In Deuteronomy 22:9-13, we come across some commandments concerning 'illicit mixtures' similar to those found in Leviticus

19:19, *"You shall keep My statutes. You shall not let your livestock breed with another kind. You shall not sow your field with mixed seed. Nor shall a garment of mixed linen and wool come upon you."*

The forbidding of women wearing men's garments and men wearing women's in Deuteronomy 22:5 is along the same lines.

The Jewish sages are not entirely sure of the reasons for these commandments and class them with the *chukkim*. *Chukkim* are decrees which are hard to understand, but God gave them so they are to be followed. However, one reason the sages give is that it is a reminder that God made distinctions in the natural world. As we have seen over and over, 'separation' is a theme throughout the Torah.

However, there is another connection made by Tom Bradford in www.torahclass.com quoted below. He makes the point that, for whatever reason God forbade the mixing of certain materials, they are symbolic of unlawful unions such as adultery, or prostitution.

'As with all illicit mixtures, the concept is that a person who is set apart for God has no business coming into union with those things or with those people who are not. To do so is an unauthorized mixture; to do so is essentially to adulterate what was pure. We not only adulterate the laws of God when we do that but we also adulterate our personal relationship WITH God'.

In the context of the theme of 'separation', the principle of guarding against being joined together with the 'unholy', has been demonstrated many times in this teaching. The

New Testament teaches the same principle concerning wrong partnerships. 1 Corinthians 6:15-16 says, *"Do you not know that your bodies are members of Christ? Shall I then take the members of Christ and make them members of a harlot? Certainly not! Or do you not know that he who is joined to a harlot is one body with her? For 'the two,' He says, 'shall become one flesh'."*

This verse is warning about an unlawful physical joining, but there are spiritual connections and partnerships too that must be avoided by God's set-apart people, and we have noted those during our studies. Let's note especially a verse we have used before in this Study, 2 Corinthians 6:14 commands us not to be unequally yoked with unbelievers because light and darkness do not mix.

Trust is essential in marriage, and suspicion or jealousy can destroy a relationship as is demonstrated in Deuteronomy 22:13-22. Marriage is considered sacred and unfaithfulness a grave sin. As we have seen before, within this provision of physical and social companionship, God embedded a beautiful picture that speaks of His desire for a faithful and intimate relationship. Unfaithfulness or suspicion in marriage destroys that picture.

Ephesians 5:25-27 uses the picture of marriage to demonstrate the relationship of Messiah and the Church, *"Husbands, love your wives, just as Christ also loved the church and gave Himself for her..."*

The theme of sexual purity continues until the end of the chapter and reinforces the principle we have seen before, that which

God created to be a beautiful gift, is to be within the boundaries of restraint.

## Deuteronomy 23
## Strive for Perfection

A note on verse 1: it is most probably a reference to men who have been connected to a heathen cult that requires a eunuch status. Or, those who may have been captured and made eunuchs. See this beautiful scripture from Isaiah 56:3-5 as an example of the grace of the LORD, "*...do not let the eunuch say, 'here I am, a dry tree.' For thus says the LORD: to the eunuchs who keep my Sabbaths, and choose what pleases Me, and hold fast to My covenant, even to them I will give in My house and within My walls a place and a name better than that of sons and daughters; I will give them an everlasting name that will not be cut off.*"

Physical abnormalities limited the roles an Israelite could undertake but they could still be part of His people. Sometimes we are limited in service because our foolish mistakes in the past have cost us opportunities, but God's grace has not changed.

Permitted and forbidden relationships are dealt with in Deuteronomy 23:3-8, and the reasons given. We have seen this principle several times in the Torah and in the New Testament. 1 Corinthians 15:33 warns, "*Do not be deceived: Evil company corrupts good habits.*"

Deuteronomy 23:9-14 is speaking of an army readying itself to do battle. In '*Lessons in Leviticus*' we looked at the laws concerning impurity in Leviticus 15 to remind ourselves that this was a serious matter in the eyes of God, and will repeat it here:

'Bodily discharges, according to the Torah of Moses, brought a person into a state of impurity. Although these are physical and even natural functions, and the rules concerning them obviously included health considerations, God is painting a definite picture for us. A person can be pure, or impure. An impurity can contaminate and cause the clean to be unclean. That which comes from <u>within</u>, wrong speech, wrong thoughts, can render us impure. Sometimes we don't even realise it. We see ourselves as right before God, but impurity which can be hidden from others, can hinder our walk with Him, and bring contamination to those with whom we fellowship. Mark 7:20-21, *"He went on: What comes out of a person is what defiles them. For it is from within, out of a person's heart, that evil thoughts come...'"*

Those whom God calls into warfare need to care about being clean before the LORD, and allow no defilement that would contaminate others. Note Deuteronomy 23:14 in which He sees that which is unclean, and turns away! What a sobering warning. Deliverance from the enemy's tactics can be thwarted by unclean lives.

It is interesting to note, along with this picture of spiritual defilement that God has embedded in His laws, the Torah is in fact, thousands of years ahead of modern understanding of sanitation and hygiene.

Although dealing with a different situation, that of disobedience and deception, the battle of Ai in Joshua chapter 7 was lost because *"...they have stolen and lied...therefore the people of Israel cannot stand before their enemies."* Joshua 7:11-12. Going into battle, literal or spiritual, requires being right before the LORD.

## Compassion

In Deuteronomy 23:15-16 there is an opportunity to note the humaneness of slavery in the Torah. Even non-Jewish slaves fleeing from injustice were to be protected. Other cultures, such as Greek and Roman, would brand runaway slaves with a hot iron. Crucifixion was also among the punishments for some infringements. In America, runaway slaves were hunted down by bloodhounds and suffered terrible punishments on top of their wretched living and working conditions. In the Land of Israel, they generally had rights. The small Book of Philemon is interesting in light of this Torah command, showing I believe, that the runaway slave Onesimus had been transformed. Master and slave, Paul believed, were now brothers in Messiah.

Deuteronomy 23:19 forbids charging interest when lending to your brother, (meaning fellow Israelites), but not to the foreigner to whom interest could be charged. The Hebrew word translated as 'foreigner' in this case is *nokri*. There are other Hebrew words for 'foreigner' or 'stranger'. One common word is *'ger'* which has the connotation of one who lives among the Jewish people and is respectful of their beliefs. Although by the Second Temple/New Testament Period this term *ger* was applied and still is, to converts to Judaism.

The '*nokri*/foreigner' was one who was not part of Israel in any way. His culture was probably very different and alien to the people of God. In fact, nokri comes from a root word, 'to be recognisable'. The kind of foreigner mentioned in this passage would have stood out in his dress or habits and would be a visiting foreigner, a trader or similar occupation where lending money would be in the category of a business deal. Ruth the Moabitess, in Ruth 2:10, described herself as a nokri.

It should be noted here that the medieval label of Jews being greedy money lenders, forever enshrined in Shakespeare's Shylock, and an association that lingers in modern minds, is therefore doubly tragic. Money lending as a way of earning a living was forced upon the Jew who, in those times, was forbidden to own land or work at many other trades.

In the last chapter of Leviticus, we talked of the seriousness of vows and here in Deuteronomy 23:21, treating a vow seriously and fulfilling it is again emphasized. Ecclesiastes 5:4-7 deals with vows and in verse 4a also emphasises, "*When you make a vow to God, do not delay to pay it.*" Back in Deuteronomy 23:18, there is a warning not to pay vows with defiled offerings.

Leviticus 19:13 says not to cheat or rob your neighbour and here in Deuteronomy 23:24 it allows one to take a little produce from your neighbour if hungry, but filling containers or using harvesting methods is really stealing. In the gospels we see Yeshua and his disciples plucking grain from someone's field. A debate developed over that action not because they were stealing, but only because it was on the Sabbath. While this is not the place to explain the context of this incident, please note

Yeshua's justification of his disciples' actions was in no way to do with changing the sanctity and status of the Sabbath.

## Deuteronomy 24
## Relationships

Although Leviticus 21:7 mentions divorce in the context of who priests could not marry, Deuteronomy 24 is the only other place in the Torah that gives another ruling concerning divorce, and that is, that a husband cannot re-marry the wife he divorced. In Jeremiah 3:1 this ruling was firmly in place as it was used by God as another example of Israel's unfaithfulness, *"They say, 'If a man divorces his wife, And she goes from him And becomes another man's, May he return to her again?' Would not that land be greatly polluted? But you have played the harlot with many lovers; Yet return to Me, says the LORD."* This verse and many others that talk of Israel defiling herself as an unfaithful, defiled wife, and the LORD as a betrayed yet faithful husband waiting for her return, is an example of the amazing grace of God.

Interestingly, conditions for divorce were still being debated at the time of Yeshua. There were two main schools of thought led by two famous scholars, one more lenient than the other regarding reasons a man could divorce his wife. It seems that Yeshua supported the more strict Rabbi, when he agreed with the stricter conditions of divorce, Matthew 19:9, *"And I say to you, whoever divorces his wife, except for sexual immorality, and marries another, commits adultery; and whoever marries her who is divorced commits adultery."*

The Mishnah[45] mentions this debate:

'The theory of the law that the husband could divorce his wife at will was challenged by the school of Shammai. It interpreted the text of Deuteronomy 24:1 in such a manner as to reach the conclusion that the husband could not divorce his wife except for cause, and that the cause must be sexual immorality'. (Gittin. ix. 10; Yer. Soṭah i.1,16b).

The Torah teaches consideration for people's feelings, for example, Deuteronomy 24:6 & 10-13 give dignity to a person in a vulnerable position. Not only were they not to be exploited when owing a debt by not taking away a man's living, but were not to be shamed in front of the man's family. Those collecting the pledge until the debt was paid could not enter his home.

The right way to treat each other in the Body of Messiah is found in the New Testament. For example, Ephesians 4:32, *"And be kind to one another, tenderhearted, forgiving one another, even as God in Christ forgave you."*

While we are in this section of scripture, compare Deuteronomy 24:8 with Luke 17: 14. Here, Yeshua was careful to follow the instructions of the Torah after the cleansing of the 'lepers'. *"So when He saw them, He said to them, 'Go, show yourselves to the priests'. And so it was that as they went, they were cleansed."*

Reread Deuteronomy 24:14-15 as it is in similar vein to most of this chapter, that is, of interacting with each other in an ethical way. But perhaps we can apply this particular verse as a

---

[45] The Mishnah, is the first work of rabbinic law, published around the year 200 CE by Rabbi Judah the Patriarch in the land of Israel.

challenge to ourselves. How often do we procrastinate in paying what is owed - do we owe thanks to someone; acknowledgement; encouragement? Sometimes we don't even realize those things are due until the moment slips away.

The chapter concludes with reminders of justice and compassion woven into the rules by which God's Set Apart People had to live.

## Deuteronomy 25
## More on Justice

A note of interest regarding verses 1-3 is that in later years there was a rabbinical ruling regarding the maximum number of blows allowed. They said it was to be no more than thirty-nine maximum, to ensure the limit was not exceeded. The flogging that Yeshua endured was at the hands of the Romans and was extremely vicious as the Romans had no such limitation and had bits of bone or lead attached to the end of the leather thongs, (NIV study notes). See Mark 15:15.

In Deuteronomy 25:5-10, what is known as a 'levirate' marriage is described. It is played out in Ruth chapter 4:5, *"Then Boaz said, 'On the day you buy the field from the hand of Naomi, you must also buy it from Ruth the Moabitess, the wife of the dead, to perpetuate the name of the dead through his inheritance'."*

In the rather bizarre scenario described in the verses 11-12 of Deuteronomy 25, it is, according to the Rabbis, not meant to be carried out literally but rather a monetary compensation.

Rashi[46] says:

'This verse is not to be understood literally, but rather, it means that she must pay monetary damages to recompense the victim for the embarrassment he suffered [through her action. The amount she must pay is calculated by the court,] all according to the [social status] of the culprit and the victim'.
[Sifrei 25:161]

In Exodus 17:8-14 is the incident concerning the Amalekites who attacked the children of Israel as they started on their journey. The LORD even told Moshe that He would blot out the remembrance of Amalek. In this passage in Deuteronomy, 24:17-19, we learn why Amalek was considered such an unscrupulous enemy: "*he... attacked your rear ranks, all the stragglers at your rear, when you were tired and weary.*" Beware of not being within a fellowship, beware of weariness.

## Deuteronomy 26
## Giving Thanks

This chapter is the beginning of a new Torah Portion/*parasha* called *Ki Tavo*/When you Come In, that is, into the land that God was giving to them. Because, it would only be when they finally entered the Promised Land, they would be able to offer the yearly First Fruits Harvest detailed in 26:1-15.

---

[46] Rabbi Shlomo Yitzhaki, (Hebrew: רבי שלמה יצחקי), better known by the acronym Rashi (February 22, 1040 – July 13, 1105), was a rabbi from France, famed as the author of the first comprehensive commentaries on the Talmud, Torah, and Tanakh (Hebrew Bible). (*Online New World Encylopedia*

We have read about this 'appointment with God' in Leviticus 23:15 where it is connected to the grain harvest and linked back to Pesach by counting the days until the 50th Day. In Numbers 28:26 it is called The Day of the First Fruits/*Hayom Bikkurim* and also mentions the grain harvest. Also several chapters back in Deuteronomy 16:9, it is called The Feast of Weeks/*Shavuot*. In this chapter, 26:1-11, all produce is included and details on how to present these first fruits to the LORD are given. It is such a beautiful acknowledgement of God's bounty. Note that harvest festivals were not unique to Israel, but only Israel recognized God as the source of the bounty and that He was there in their history. The different stages of harvest are celebrated and linked to some historical event of importance, for example, Passover is associated with the exodus from Egypt.

In 26:12-19, after the people set aside all their tithes, in other words that which belongs to the LORD, He affirms His special relationship with them. When we honour Him, He elevates us, perhaps not in the world's eyes, but in His. It is interesting to note the repeat of the word 'today'. This repetition also occurs in Deuteronomy 26:16, 17, 18; 27:1; 29:4 & 13. Note the emphasis on 'today' in verses 16-19. Serving Him was not to be put off to a later time but be an ongoing action as would be His blessings. However, there is another thought that 'this day', or 'today' means understanding the significance of being part of God's treasure/*segula*, of taking hold of the day – each day - the LORD has given us. *"This is the day that the LORD has made, we will rejoice and be glad in it."* Psalm 118:24.

## Deuteronomy 27 & 28
## Blessings or Curses

These chapters of blessings and curses are a dramatic portrayal of the consequences of choices in regard to following the ways of God - or not following. They provide an obvious principle. God will lift His blessing when we wilfully ignore Him, even while He waits in His mercy to receive us back.

For your interest, *Rosh Hashanah,* as the Feast of Trumpets is called today, marks the beginning of a solemn time of introspection and repentance before the Day of Atonement ten days later. Before Rosh Hashanah though, the Jewish people are required to read this list of curses. It is certainly a sobering check list of moral and ethical standards.

## Deuteronomy 29
## It's All about Choice

We come to the ending of what began in chapter 1 when Moses began to expound on the Torah. His speech was after the defeat of powerful kings and the nation was poised to enter a new phase in their life. He recalled for them their wanderings, their victories and failures, and emphasized the importance of obedience over and over. Now Moshe is nearing the end of his 37-day exhortation, and he again recaps their journey and mentions the defeat of Sihon and Og of whom he had spoken about in chapter 3:1-2. Chapter 29:2-9 are reminders of trials, battles and miracles. His listeners were mostly the second generation who had not witnessed the same things their parents did.

The theme of 'Choice and its Consequences' continues! Deuteronomy 29:10 is a picture of the nation standing before God that includes <u>everyone</u>, different roles and levels of authority but equal before God. It says to us that it is the responsibility of all in the family of God to hear from Him with understanding and commitment.

Moshe recognizes the tendency of humans to be curious. Curiosity is one of those things which is both our strength and our weakness. Curiosity has led to a multitude of positive discoveries but, as 29:16-19 reveals, it can lead to looking into that which is forbidden and certainly harmful. It can lead to delusion which has us stubbornly following our own way thinking that we can retain spiritual peace, (verse 19). Curiosity can also result in idolatry which in any form is a trap that turns one away from wholeheartedly following God. 1 John 5:21, *"Little children, keep yourselves from idols."* Proverbs 3:7 gives good advice too, *"be not wise in your own eyes; fear the LORD and depart from evil."*

Deception can come in many guises: Colossians 2:8, *"Beware lest anyone cheat you through philosophy and empty deceit, according to the tradition of men, according to the basic principles of the world, and not according to Christ."*

Deuteronomy 29:29 ends the chapter emphasising our responsibility before God. There may be things we will never understand <u>or are not meant to understand</u>. But that which He

**has** revealed to us is to enable us to live in obedience to His word. Let us be careful to be accountable in what we know, and not be caught up in fruitless speculations about things that are not yet revealed or are yet to come, which can lead to division and distraction.

## Deuteronomy 30
### It's Easy to Obey

Something interesting to note is that verse 3 speaks of the regathering of the Jewish people, and it is the 5,708[th] verse in Hebrew in the Five Books of Moses. The year 5708, according to the Hebrew calendar dating, corresponds with 1948, the year of the rebirth of Modern Israel.

Yes, among the dire warnings of the consequences of disobedience, there is the promise of restoration. It is a promise being fulfilled in our day concerning the restored nation of Israel, with full spiritual restoration yet to come. We can also hold to that promise, when we, or our loved ones, are in a far place from God, 30:2-5 - He can restore! However, the word translated as 'return' in 30:2 - *shuv* - can also mean 'repentance' or 'turn back'. With this meaning, the first step therefore, is to turn away from sin and face the direction back to God.

So much in Moshe's exhortations to this second generation is about choice. God's directions for holy living are for us to choose, reject, or merely neglect. We have free will. God did not create robots. The 2018 commentary from the Temple Institute in Jerusalem says this in relation to chapters 29-30:

'When G-d first created Adam, and set him in the Garden of Eden, He assigned man the task of tending to and guarding over the Garden of Eden. Man was free to do as he pleased, save for one negative commandment, one 'No!' and that, of course, was eating from the Tree of Knowledge. The 'No' was absolute and non-negotiable, but contained in G-d's 'No' was the potential to choose to defy G-d's will, and, by doing so, the birth of man's free will. G-d's response to the flowering of man's free will over the generations was Torah, G-d's gift to Israel at Sinai, whose every commandment and every insight is predicated on man's free will. Choosing "to love HaShem, your G-d, to walk in His ways, and to observe His commandments, His statutes, and His ordinances," (Deut. 30:16) as expressed at the conclusion of *Parashat Nitzavim*, is the heart and soul of Torah, G-d's covenant with man, the master of free will. Choose G-d's ways and the Garden of Eden is yours to tend to and guard over. Choose a path that is not G-d's, and thorns and thistles await you'.

While the last verse of Deuteronomy 29 speaks of secret things belonging to the LORD, His commandments have been made very clear. We have no excuses according to Deuteronomy 30:11-14. Paul uses this scripture in connection to belief in Messiah Yeshua, in Romans 10:5-9. Just as the Torah was clearly given from heaven, so the gospel message that Messiah has been revealed has also been made clear, *"for Moses writes about the righteousness which is of the law, 'The man who does those things shall live by them.' But the righteousness of faith speaks in this way, 'Do not say in your heart, 'Who will ascend into heaven?' (that is, to bring Christ down from above) or, 'Who will descend into the abyss?' (that is, to bring Christ up from the dead). But what does it say? 'The word is near you, in your mouth and in your heart' (that is, the word of faith which we preach): that if you confess with your mouth the Lord Jesus and believe in your heart that God has raised Him from the dead, you will be saved.*"

Deuteronomy 30:15-20 is again about the theme that looms large for His set-apart people, **choice!** From these verses: life and good, death and evil; choose life, Moshe implores!

The Bible teaches a dynamic faith and Deuteronomy 30:20 is an example: <u>love</u> God; <u>obey</u> his voice; <u>cling</u> to Him. All words of action, and choice. The reason is to dwell within all God has promised, to remain in His will and in the security of knowing He is for us. Proverbs 3:1-2 endorses these inspiring words, *"My son, do not forget my law, But let your heart keep my commands; For length of days and long life and peace they will add to you."* Perhaps a key to not forgetting is this verse from Psalm 119:11, *"Your word I have hidden in my heart, That I might not sin against You."*

## Deuteronomy 31
## Accepting Changes

In verse 1 Moshe states his age, 120 years old. He fulfilled the new ideal which God ordained in Genesis 6:3 before the flood that man could live to 120 years, rather than for the long periods of time that early generations lived. This is why a Jewish birthday greeting is to wish the recipient, *'ad mea v'esrim'*. (May you live to 120!)

Moshe in this chapter is concluding his long exhortations of choice and consequences in regard to obeying the LORD with whom they are in covenant. So, let's continue to note some beautiful principles.

Within verses 1-15, Moshe hands the leadership over to Yehoshua whereby Moshe remains a great role model in leadership. He accepts that God is bringing his long role as deliverer and leader to an end and honours the new leader, God's choice, in front of the nation, Deuteronomy 31:7, with beautiful words of encouragement.

Even though he was the good age of 120 years, he was not feeble as we read in Deuteronomy 34:7, "*His eyes were not dim nor his natural vigour diminished.*" So he was still physically capable of leading his people and as we know, had begged God to allow him to continue. However, we see that it is God who brings eras in a person's life to an end, and we must accept His timing as Moshe did. He not only accepted His timing but His choice. Jewish commentary wonders how Moshe felt about his sons not succeeding him, but they acknowledge that this demonstrated that serving God is not dependent on birth and privilege, but anyone with the right heart can be used by Him in the role He chooses for that person.

Another wonderful lesson in this narrative is the beautiful assurance that God will not forsake us. As they entered a new phase of their journey which was not just a physical one, but also a spiritual one, Moshe assures them that the LORD will never leave them or forsake them, Deuteronomy 31:6. He used the same words to encourage Yehoshua in his new role and Deuteronomy 31:8 and Hebrews 13:5 quote those words in the context of being content with God's provision and not be consumed with money making. *"Let your conduct be without covetousness; be content with such things as you have. For He Himself has said, "I will never leave you nor forsake you."* In both Scripture passages, it is about trusting God's promises.

Another principle to take to heart is not to forget God's Divine Instructions, as individuals and as a collective Body. In Deuteronomy 31:10-13, Moshe issues one final instruction from the LORD concerning the end of the seventh year, the 'year of release', and that was for everyone to come together to hear the words of the LORD as the Torah was read to them.

The 'year of release' meant the *'shmita'*, the year in which the land lies fallow about which we learned in *'Lessons from Leviticus'* (Leviticus 25:3-4).

Gathering together to hear this Book of Instruction read every seven years was re-established in modern Israel, and is known as the *Hakhel* ceremony, 'a gathering together'. At the time of writing this Study, the last one was sukkot, 2015. The reason for hearing the Word of God is spelt out in 31:12-13, *"to learn to fear...God and carefully guard and keep the words of His Torah, His guide for a holy life."*

## Deuteronomy 32
## The Song of Moses, Redemption Guaranteed

Moshe receives a most discouraging message from the LORD, that after his death, the people of Israel will turn away from their God and embrace idolatry and suffer the consequences,

Deuteronomy 31:16-18. The Song that God gives Moshe therefore, is a Song of Redemption. What grace and what hope in its words!

The song recounts what will happen, their turning away, their chastisement via the nations and then God's punishment of those nations, and finally gives a promise that atonement will be provided.

Because the Torah urges that *"in the mouth of two or three witnesses let every word be established…"* Deuteronomy 19:15 (and endorsed in Matthew 18:16), Moshe calls on two witnesses in 33:1 - the heaven and the earth. The prophet Isaiah does the same in Isaiah 1:2 when he is about to bring a long rebuke from the LORD, *"Hear O heavens and give ear O earth."*

In Deuteronomy 32:1 Moshe wants his words to be as penetrating as the rain, and yet as gentle as the dew.

The song goes on to tell of the Israelites status before God, their faithlessness and of God's faithfulness. It is a witness against them in the case of blaming God when things go wrong and He withdraws His presence for a time [lit. – 'hides His face'] 31:18. It is not God at fault because Deuteronomy 32:4 tells us that He is without injustice, righteous.

Our God is the Rock says verse 4, and there are different Hebrew words that can be translated 'rock'. In this verse it is the word *'tsur'* - the kind of rock that is towering, majestic, immovable.

A perfect and righteous God stands in contrast to His corrupt and foolish people in verses 5-6. They even separate themselves from their Father because of their sin, *"...they are not His children because of their blemish..."* This is a significant point because they have the privilege of being a set aside people, (verses 7-9). The song reminds them of a loving Father and Redeemer, and from verses 10-14 we have a most poignant account of His redemption and care of Israel.

Ezekiel 16:1-20 echoes the love and heartbreak of God over His people in a similar manner, for example. *"No eye pitied you, to do any of these things for you, to have compassion on you; but you were thrown out into the open field, when you yourself were loathed on the day you were born. And when I passed by you and saw you struggling in your own blood, I said to you in your blood, 'Live!' Yes, I said to you in your blood, 'Live!' I made you thrive like a plant in the field; and you grew, matured, and became very beautiful."* Ezekiel 16:5-7

I'm sorry to bring a little disillusionment about the soaring eagle (*nesher*) in God's dramatic picture of carrying His people to great heights in Deuteronomy 32: 11-13. Unfortunately, *nesher* is not an eagle but it is a vulture, a Griffin vulture[47]. And although we don't think of a vulture in the same way as the more noble eagle, at least in our eyes, in fact the ancient world wasn't bothered by it, as the Griffin vulture is a magnificent bird with a wingspan up to 2.4 metres/eight feet and is the highest flying bird.

In verse 15 is the first use of the word 'Yeshurun' in the Torah. As it comes from the root *yashar* meaning upright, it is an ironic choice. *Yeshurun* was one of their names bestowed by their

---

[47] Torah Encyclopaedia of the Animal Kingdom; Rabbi Natan Slifkin.

Father, but rather than remain upright, they would be led astray by the influence of their idolatrous neighbours, Deuteronomy 32:16-18. In 32:19-26, harsh discipline of the LORD would follow.

We know from the Books of History and the Prophets in the Bible, that God used nations as His tools of discipline. However, He also comes to the aid of His nation, as in verses 32:26-27. They may not deserve His help, in fact they at times deserved obliteration from memory, but their enemies who were only tools in the Hand of the LORD, would think it was they who caused the humiliation of Israel. The nations never realised that the victories over Israel they enjoyed, were only because God allowed them. Usually, they very enthusiastically carried out their undisclosed, but God-given role, to the point where they were in turn punished for their harsh treatment of His nation. God will take vengeance on their enemies and provide atonement for His people and His Land.

Note the commandment at the beginning of Deuteronomy 32:43 to the Gentiles, to rejoice with His people. It is one that is not only ignored, but instead, negative and even hateful attitudes are directed towards the People and the Land. Back in Exodus 18:9, when Moshe's father-in-law came to the camp of Israel, it says, *"then Jethro rejoiced for all the good which the LORD had done for Israel..."* May this once pagan priest be a role model.

There have been other beautiful 'songs' in the Hebrew Scriptures, such as 2 Samuel 22:1-51. However, we find this Song, given by God but known as the Song of Moses, still sung in Revelation 15:3. *"And I saw something like a sea of glass mingled with fire, and those who have the victory over the beast, over his image and over his mark and over the number of his name, standing on the sea of glass, having harps of God. They sing the song of Moses, the servant of God, and the song of the Lamb, saying: 'Great and marvelous are Your works, Lord God Almighty! Just and true are Your ways, O King of the saints! Who shall not fear You, O Lord, and glorify Your name? For You alone are holy. For all nations shall come and worship before You, For Your judgments have been manifested'.*" Two songs proclaiming redemption!

## Deuteronomy 33
## Blessings

In 33:1-5 Moshe begins with the light that shone on them at Mt Sinai. That light was the Torah given in fire for all of Israel. And although the Torah was specifically to the 'Tribes of Israel', the LORD's love embraces all peoples, as we know. For example, Psalm 145:9, "*The LORD is good to all, And His tender mercies are over all His works.*" This study on the treasures of Torah has endeavoured to demonstrate that although part of the Torah often called the 'Mosaic Law', was delivered from God Himself on Mt Sinai to the Jewish nation, His other 'set apart ones' can also receive His words, not with the obligation to keep all the commandments/*mitzvot* literally, but to absorb the teaching, the principles, patterns and pictures embedded therein.

The Blessings of each tribe generally refer to their inheritance in the Promised Land and contain prophetic aspects. We will note some things of interest. Deuteronomy 33:6 was a prayer that Reuben not diminish. Interestingly, in the first census in Numbers 1:21 the tribe numbered 46,500 men but in the second in Numbers 26:7, the number was 43,730. In the time of King David much of the territory they had chosen in which to settle was conquered by the Moabites.

The tribe of Levi was not given their own tribal portion but were to be given cities with some land within tribal boundaries. However, they were given a tremendous spiritual blessing with the responsibility of the priesthood. This is a good time for God's royal and holy priesthood, see 1 Peter 2:5 and 9, to check those obligations by looking at the positive words of blessing spoken over this tribe and applying them in a spiritual sense. Deuteronomy 33:9 speaks of priorities, that is, obedience to God coming before every other loyalty. The next verse, 10, is about sharing God's word and offering worship.

Just as Benjamin/*Benyamin*, was a beloved son of his father Yakov, Deuteronomy 33:12 echoes that parental love in God's love for that tribe. His nearness and protection spoken of in this verse meant that Benyamin's territory would include part of the temple area according to rabbinical tradition.

Proceeding to Deuteronomy 33:19, it was well known that Zebulon's tribe participated in maritime activities, hence the reference to 'the abundance of the seas'. The 'treasures hidden in the sand' can refer, it is thought, to glass making which according to Josephus and other Jewish writings took place on the sands of Acre/*Acco*.

Take time to read and absorb the poetic and profound last verses of this chapter. Deuteronomy 33:26-29: The Eternal was their Shelter, their Supporter, their Defender, their Provider. A unique people, belonging to a unique God. The God to whom through His mercy, we can also belong.

*"...that you were at that time separate from Messiah, alienated from the commonwealth of Yisra'el, and strangers from the covenants of the promise, having no hope and without God in the world. But now in Messiah Yeshua you who once were far off are made near in the blood of Messiah."* Ephesians 2:12-13 HNV.

## Deuteronomy 34
## Poised on the Brink of a New Beginning

God ensured that there would no grave for Moshe so there would be no shrine. His servant Moshe died pointing the people towards Joshua and away from himself in the way that John/ *Yochanan* the Baptizer did towards Yeshua. Let Hebrews 3:5 have the final word about Moshe, *"And Moses indeed was faithful in all His house as a servant, for a testimony of those things which would be spoken afterward..."*

*I delight to do Your will, O my God, and Your Torah is within my heart. Psalm 40:8*

Yeshua declared, *"Do not think that I came to destroy the Law (Torah) or the Prophets. I did not come to destroy them but to fulfil them."* Matthew 5:17. The Greek word translated as 'fulfil', is *'pleroo'* and means to obey the law/Torah to the full as well as exemplify its full meaning. We have gleaned much from the rich fields of Torah in order to apply some of that meaning to our lives. There is more to be revealed as you continue to explore and learn.

# ABOUT THE AUTHOR

Maxine has a unique insight into the value of the Old Testament for Christians. As a keen student of the Bible for over 40 years, Maxine has devoted much of that time to learning how the ancient Judaic riches of the early part of the Bible still offer powerful meaning for contemporary Christians. Known for her insightful teachings as a Bible Study leader, and speaker at Israel-related events, Maxine is passionate about enabling Christians to have a better understanding of their Christian roots, in order to deepen their faith. Maxine has spent over 20 years living in Israel while working as a volunteer, along with her husband, where her appreciation of the importance of the Torah in the lives of all who follow the God of Israel has grown. In this book Maxine combines the wisdom from both Christian understanding, and Jewish Scholarship, to support a deeper connection with the Torah in the Christian world.